KT-217-936

# One Man and his Dog

PHIL DRABBLE

PELHAM BOOKS/Stephen Greene Press

PELHAM BOOKS/Stephen Greene Press
Published by the Penguin Group
27 Wrights Lane, London W8 5TZ, England
Viking Penguin Inc., 40 West 23rd Street, New York, New York 10010, USA
The Stephen Greene Press, 15 Muzzey Street, Lexington, Massachusetts 02173, USA
Penguin Books Australia Ltd, Ringwood, Victoria, Australia
Penguin Books Canada Ltd, 2801 John Street, Markham, Ontario, Canada L3R 1B4
Penguin Books (NZ) Ltd, 182–190 Wairau Road, Auckland 10, New Zealand

Penguin Books Ltd, Registered Offices: Harmondsworth, Middlesex, England

First published 1989

Copyright © Phil Drabble 1989

All rights reserved. Without limiting the rights under copyright
reserved above, no part of this publication may be reproduced, stored
in or introduced into a retrieval system, or transmitted, in any
form or by any means (electronic, mechanical, photocopying,
recording or otherwise), without the prior written permission of
both the copyright owner and the above publisher of this book

Typeset in 11/13 pt Photina and
Printed and bound in Great Britain by Butler & Tanner Ltd, Frome and London

ISBN 0 7207 1878 3

A CIP catalogue record for this book is available from the British Library

*Illustration credits*

With the exception of the photographs on pages 154, 156 and 157 which are
reproduced by permission of the BBC and those on pages 89, 103, 137 and 150
which are reproduced by permission of Derek Johnson all the photographs were
supplied by Sally Anne Thompson and R.T. Willbie of Animal Photography. The
cartoon on page 5 is by Larry, the one on page 181 is by MAC and is reproduced by
permission of the artist and the *Daily Mail* and the one on page 183 is by Cole.

# Contents

*Also by Phil Drabble*

Staffordshire (*Hales County Books 1948*)
Black Country (*Hales regional Books 1952*)
Of Pedigree Unknown (*Cassell 1964*)
A Weasel in my Meatsafe (*Collins 1957*)
The Penguin Book of Pets (*Penguin 1964*)
Badgers at my Window (*Pelham 1969*)
My Beloved Wilderness (*Pelham 1971*)
Design for a Wilderness (*Pelham 1973*)
Pleasing Pets (*William Luscombe 1975*)
Phil Drabble's Book of Pets (*Fontana 1976*)
Phil Drabble's Country Scene (*Pelham 1974*)
Phil Drabble's Country Seasons (*Michael Joseph 1976*)
Countrywise (*Michael Joseph 1980*)
Country Matters (*Michael Joseph 1982*)
Country Moods (*Michael Joseph 1985*)
No Badgers in My Wood (*Michael Joseph 1979*)
One Man and His Dog (*Michael Joseph 1978*)
What Price the Countryside? (*Michael Joseph 1985*)
My Wilderness in Bloom (*Michael Joseph 1986*)
Of Pedigree Unknown (*Huddlesford Publications 1987*)

# Foreword

TELEVISION HAS AN insatiable appetite and in the hundreds and hundreds of hours of programmes that are fed annually to the viewers with the countless presenters, performers and experts parading across our screens, there is always a cherished moment when a 'character' comes into our homes with his own individual charm and quiet authority. Such a man is Phil Drabble.

Unmistakable in his cloth cap and tweed jacket, Phil has now notched up his one hundredth recording of *One Man and His Dog*. He has introduced every single programme since the series first began back in 1975 and, with Eric Halsall, has watched something like three hundred and fifty trials, met and chatted to countless shepherds and farmers and listened avidly to tales from country folk. Phil has always had enormous respect for the competitors in *One Man and His Dog* and all of us who work closely on the programme know them as very dedicated and likeable people.

In this delightful new book, Phil Drabble tells us of the early days of the programme, of its development and of its expansion. He elaborates upon many of the incidents that have occurred during the thirteen years the programme has been running and, drawing from his vast knowledge of the countryside and all matters concerned with conservation, he expresses his personal and strongly held views, sometimes controversial, on matters that have a related interest to sheep dogs, livestock and country matters.

With years as a broadcaster, countryman and author behind him, Phil has brought his combined talents to the television programme that has almost a cult following. Indeed it is a fact that national newspapers, magazines and weekend colour supplements have latched onto the programme for feature articles and their cartoonists have found unlimited material with which to amuse their readers. So whether they be people bred and brought up in the agricultural surroundings of the shires and the dales, or city commuters living in high-rise flats and modern suburbia, *One Man and His Dog* has brought them moments on television to savour and, with his distinctive style of story telling, Phil Drabble's new book will prove to be a most welcome companion.

His enthusiasm and passion for the countryside and the programme are etched into every chapter and leave the reader feeling totally involved with the making of the series and acquainted with both the people who compete with their dogs in front of the cameras and with those who bring it to the television screens.

Ian Smith

# 1
# Genesis

THE LONG running success of the television sheep dog programme *One Man and His Dog* is largely due to luck.

It began with a splash of bad luck. Philip Gilbert, the first producer, was on holiday in Northumberland one sobbing wet week in 1974 and he called in at a local agricultural show out of curiosity. There were a crowd of soaked spectators in one corner of the field, watching a minor sheep dog trial and, never having seen one before, he not only joined them to see what the attraction was, but began to chat them up.

Television producers are forever on the look-out for something which is different from – and if possible better than – the current fare on the small screen. This was certainly different! Competitor after competitor moved a bunch of sheep round the obstacles on a formalised course, simply by whistling coded commands to his shaggy dog. The enthusiasm of the soggy spectators was infectious, their country brogue attractive and the intelligence of their dogs truly enthralling. The sheer luck of having dropped in by chance on this rural minor sport burned an image on the back of his mind which wouldn't go away. So when he saw that the Supreme International Sheep Dog Trials were to be held at Leek, in Staffordshire, Philip Gilbert decided that nothing would keep him away.

Although I am so Staffordshire bred-and-born that friends say I need a passport out of my native county, I would be the last to claim that Leek has many visual attractions. I gather that the International, that year, was held on a field as flat as a football pitch, with factories as a backcloth. Any normal television producer would have turned tail and fled home or into the nearest hostelry.

Not so Philip. He watched for a bit and listened to the commentary over the public address system, which was punctuated by praise for this or that 'wisest dog on earth', with eulogies about 'these wonderful hill dogs' – which were playing animated chess, with sheep as pawns, on a dull field at the back of beyond.

The incongruities between the billowing enthusiasm of the commentator and the undistinguished scenery fired the determination of the man from the BBC to meet the voice behind the microphone. He turned out to be Eric Halsall, who has done the commentary on every trial, in every series of *One Man and His Dog*, for the ensuing thirteen years.

While he was there, Philip Gilbert took a few photographs – but the camera was so far from the seat of operations that the miniscule men and dogs on film seemed no larger than tomtits perched on a round of beef.

It was not an auspicious beginning. A very wet minor trial, followed by the creme-de-la-creme of international sheep dog dramas – played out on a dreary semi-urban stage. The one bright spot was that Eric Halsall was such a dyed-in-the-wool addict for anything connected with sheep or sheep dogs that the producer caught an incurable dose of his enthusiasm.

While still 'high' on the experience, he put up the idea to his controller for a pilot programme to show that a sheep dog trial might catch viewers' imagination.

The next slice of luck was that he discovered that he had breathed a puff of life into a monster which he could not control. He was hoist with his own petard.

The reply from the controller agreed that sheep dog trials were an excellent idea, so Philip was landed with the task, of producing not one pilot programme, which could be swept under the carpet in the least popular of viewing times if it did not work, but with a series of seven thirty-five minute programmes, which could leave him with enough egg on his face to obliterate his career if he made a hash of them. There was nothing for it but to get down to the nitty-gritty of the most detailed planning.

The strong card was that Eric was such a single track sheep and dog fanatic that it is said that wool, not hair, sprouts from his head. He eats, drinks, sleeps and thinks sheep and sheep dogs. He goes to trials every Saturday and sends reports of results to the farming press on Sunday. His wife is a sheep dog widow.

Although he had experience as an agricultural journalist, he had never worked before a television camera. So the producer looked round for someone to present and link the programme who had done similar jobs before, preferably with a rural background who was on beam with dogs and dog-men.

I had been on – and off! – the small screen since the early 1950s and had been brought up with dogs and dog-men. As a kid of eleven I was owned by a terrier whose distinguishing feature was a brown patch on her head. She enjoyed widespread fame as a slaughterer of rats. Her mother was a neat little smooth-coated fox terrier which, judging by the size and ugliness of my pup's head, had had a street accident with a bull terrier. But inelegance is only skin deep, for deeds leave deeper impressions than such minor blemishes. Nobody had ever heard of me, but I was widely known as 'the kid wot belongs to the lemon-eyed bitch'.

Such dogs are the perfect introduction to all genuine countrymen. 'Hairy' Kelly, our local ratcatcher, was a cunning little bachelor who had his way with rats. Those who stood within yards downwind could comprehend why he was a bachelor – but all was forgiven by anyone who witnessed his craft at catching rats! His long arms reached to his knees so that, with his hirsute aspect and unwashed shirt and skin, he resembled an orang-utan. But he had the reflexes of a Test wicket-keeper and could pick up rats, in his hands, as fast as the ferrets bolted them. Having captured them alive, he wasted no time finding a receptacle to contain them. He simply stuffed them down the neck of his shirt, having first tightened his belt to make sure that they did not creep down further than was comfortable. When no more quarry were left to bolt, he groped around his midriff, extracting fugitive rat after rat, to be deposited in a sack which was his sales-counter in the local pub at night. His customers were fellow boozers, who bought live rats to train their pups, or invested their week's wages in bets to decide whose dog could catch ten or a score of rats the quickest.

He didn't really like me – or, to be more accurate, my dog – because, however quick his reflexes, she was even quicker on her rat. When her jaws closed upon it, it was unsaleable as quarry in the rat pit, so that, even if he claimed overall responsibility for removing vermin, he only got paid once for its capture and not a second time when sold alive to gambling clients. Nevertheless, he tolerated my presence. He tended to be rather light fingered so that, after his departure, it was not always only rats which were reported missing. This resulted in

3

sales resistance to his return, but he had the ingratiating manner of the curate currying favour with the squire. 'Oh! Let me come, sir,' he would whinge, 'I've got the doctor's son with me and I've promised to show him how to go on!'

I may say that the doctor's son, by the age of twelve or thirteen, knew far more about 'how to go on' than was acceptable, in polite society. But an education by Hairy and his highly practical like taught me far more about 'how to go on' than any academic school gaffer with knobbly knees and a butterfly net. It was the perfect way for a lad to learn his natural history and to get on level terms with the type of country 'characters' who are popularly supposed to be extinct – but who I believe were never common, or they would not have stood out as 'characters'.

Nor have I ever been without a 'working' dog – and I still feel half dressed if I am forced to leave my current canine companion at home. I have had ratting dogs and whippets, lurchers for catching hares, and Alsatians for catching poachers. They all arrive at about eight weeks old and stay, as honoured members of the household, 'til death us do part. Perhaps the favourite of all was Tick, a German Short Haired Pointer, who shared my life for twelve happy years. My current constant companion is Nip, a mongrel Alsatian, who first caught my eye in an outrageously cheeky advert for 'Pedigree-cross Alsatians'.

Each, in her own way, has been the perfect introduction to a whole magnum of delightful countrymen. A stranger, with an obviously sensible, well trained dog, cannot be all bad, whether he works within the law or sails close to the rural wind. Such a common bond sparks off a relationship of mutual trust – and the owner of such a pooch is often of sufficient interest to more conventional folk, who could never inspire his confidence themselves.

When Philip Gilbert 'discovered' sheep dog trialling and, with it, Eric Halsall, the arch-commentator on the little known sport, it so happened that I had been introducing several rural programmes in which previously unknown countrymen had figured. So Philip Gilbert 'phoned to invite me to present his proposed series on Sheep Dog Trials.

My instinct was to decline politely and, if pressed, to tell this enthusiastic BBC producer to get lost. The spectacle of a lone figure, pinpointed on a bare hillside with an undistinguished shaggy dog, did not seem to me to be the ideal bait to seduce peak television audiences. Visions of shepherds issuing endless, indecipherable blasts on unmusical whistles simply turned me off. So I reckoned that hardboiled urban audiences

would find sheep doggery so repetitious that they would soon switch to something more dramatic or violent or lascivious, on other channels. Men in my profession are rated as good – or as bad! – as their last programme, and it is easier to fall headlong down the ladder of fame than it is to climb up it. Joining a commentator I had never heard of, to work for a producer I didn't know, in such a chanccy venture, seemed a totally uncommercial risk. So I followed my instinct and declined, with thanks.

Such producers do not easily take No for an answer. He said that the least I could do would be to meet him and Eric before I turned the offer down. 'Why not come and have lunch with us?' he invited, 'and go into it in more depth.' Sensing a high powered hospitality lunch, in London, I accepted. I thought I'd go – if only for the beer! – but I miscalculated. 'Right,' he said, 'Eric lives in Lancashire and you live in Staffordshire. We'll meet half-way, at Knutsford. It will keep down the expenses!'

5

It was not what I'd had in mind, but I was trapped. We met in a grotty little boozer in Knutsford, where the beer was flat and the cheese was hard, and the traffic outside the window unbearable. Everything was against us – but Eric and I discovered we were totally on beam before there was time to rejoice that we had finished our tepid pints. It was the old story of dogs being the perfect introduction to other dog-men – though we had both left our dogs at home! Our common interest conquered our caution, and the slick London producer smooth-tongued us into having a go. He was, indeed, a smooth talker. He said he'd taken on board the legitimate criticism that the programme could be repetitious, but he thought Eric's bubbling enthusiasm would put across the mystique of such a specialist sport in jargon which urbanites would grasp.

We were all agreed that television is too ofen a prostitute which exploits unnatural appetites for sex, politics and violence; that only bad news and 'establishment'-knocking interviews, where decency is derided, are considered by the trendies in news and current affairs programmes to be likely to 'amuse' sophisticated viewers. So we hoped our programme would be rated better – and we were determined it would be different!

The plan would be to open up to a background of simply stunning scenery, which would not only be beautiful but also peaceful and secluded. We would make uncommitted viewers, switching on, not knowing what to expect, sit up and say, 'Thank God for something wholesome, for a change.' They would absorb the view, and it would take their breath away. It was decided, therefore, that the first pro-gramme would be held at Buttermere, with white sheep moving against a blue lake, with towering crags in contrast with the peace.

Television is a ruthless medium, which sorts out the fakes and wide-boys, as all who suffer interminable Party Political Broadcasts and slick 'experts', whose object is to make honest folk look stupid, will know. The shepherds who join us in our programmes come across as the real men they are. They are out in all weathers in wild places, tending their sheep with the skill and sympathy which have not changed for thousands of years. They are courteous but tough and independent – all qualities which are rare in our society, ridden with get-rich-at-any-price tycoons and bureaucrats and skivers. Our shepherds are Nature's gentlemen, in the best sense. I rate it as a great privilege to meet them, and so, I find, do our viewers.

Their dogs are equally delightful. All nice people like nice dogs, and it is an especial treat to meet dogs which will do something our dogs could not do.

To set the scene for that first series, it was decided to visit a shepherd on a remote hill farm to show him at work, in the sort of conditions that would shrivel effete townsfolk's guts to raffia. I was summoned to appear at Tim Longton's farm, in the hills above Lancaster, the following Monday morning.

I got a nasty shock. Most of my previous experience on the box was on regional television, where a 'reporter' went on assignments with a cameraman and his assistant and a sound engineer. If it was something really 'important', there might be an electrician – or 'sparks' – to provide necessary ancillary lighting. Such dignitaries as Producers and Directors and Personal Assistants were luxuries for the big timers from London, undreamed of in our horse-and-buggy regional backwoods.

When I arrived at the Longton's farm I walked into the full treatment. Philip Gilbert was very much in charge and, as I had got on fine with him at the meeting with Eric in the Knutsford pub, that was very reassuring. The camera crew, consisting of a cameraman and his assistant, sound engineer and 'sparks' were smart city slickers, obviously decked out in all the gear they imagine local yokels wear. Bright anoraks and blue denim jeans and woolly hats were *de rigueur*. Highly coloured golfing umbrellas were much in evidence and they certainly lent colour to the drab grey rocks and russet bracken and dowdy heather of inhospitable hills, however out of place they looked. But the biggest shock was the producer's Personal Assistant, a fireball of a wench, who never put two feet on the ground at the same time and rarely stopped talking. I wished I was at home.

Tim Longton and his family were delightful. Our mutual involvement with working dogs, though of very different breeds, put us immediately in tune. I understood what he was talking about and he seemed relieved that I did not bombard him with stupid questions. 'Dog-men' of all ages and types are instantly recognisable by other dog-men, as certainly as one freemason reacts to the handshake of any brother on the square.

We filmed Tim Longton up in the hills, using his dogs to bring sheep down from their grazing on slopes unclimbable by mortal man. Anyone foolish enough to try would have started a minor avalanche among the shifty, rocky scree, and been decanted, bruised and battered, hundreds of feet below. Tim showed us a young dog, in training, herding docile ducks, right and left, as commanded by his whistle.

*Timothy Longton before his brace trial. His run in the 1987 semi-final was said by the judges to be the best brace run they'd ever seen.*

To get 'reverse angles' – or shots of the shepherd watching the stock he was controlling – which were out of view of the camera, Simon Betts, the young 'stage manager' in the prestigious crew, cavorted around where the sheep were (in theory!), so that Tim's eyes focused

8

in the precise direction to make the sequence convincing to future viewers.

That young stage manager is now the distinguished producer of such programmes as the sophisticated *Come Dancing*. I often wonder if he recalls the day he gambolled in remote hill country, imitating wayward sheep, in the virtuous cause of making perfection even more perfect, when the camera sequence brought sheep and working sheep dogs into the nation's living rooms.

Meanwhile, the producer's personal assistant not only never stopped talking but created a one-girl double act by not stopping writing either. She had a clipboard on which she recorded, in numerical order, every shot in every sequence. Not only did she record them, but she was full of highly technical jargon, prompting the producer if she thought there was the least chance the shots his cameraman was taking would not edit together smoothly. If there is anything that really turns me off, it is an efficient woman. What made this one even worse was that she was nearly always right!

Belonging to the persuasion whose creed is 'some you win and some you lose', I told my wife when I got home that my experience at Lancaster was not among my finest hours and that I was appalled by the prospect of being hived-up in some god-forsaken pub in the hills with a bevy of sophisticates with whom I had nothing in common, for the best part of a week. Before that happened, I was required to turn up at Television Centre, the Mecca of TV meccas, to 'dub' commentary on the film recorded at Tim Longton's.

When the programme started, thirteen years ago, the victims were still in a studio, furnished with a desk and television screen. Film was then played on the screen by the producer, who sat watching through a glass window from an adjacent studio, crammed with sophisticated gadgetry, and operated by technical staff. The producer determined the duration of the shots to be shown – and the victim was expected to write a script for the spiel he would deliver, to be dubbed on as sound to fit the pictures.

Every paragraph or so, the film was wound back while the victim spouted his piece to see if it matched the silent pictures on the screen. If it did, the film was spooled on and the process was repeated. If speech didn't synchronise with vision, the text was amended so that the victim would have another go.

When all went well, and it was the most boringly finicky operation imaginable, it took half a day or more to lay sound onto quite short films. When things went wrong, short fuses were lit and tempers detonated.

Things are better now that so much is recorded on videotape, which can be played back in the comfort of an office – or even at home – with no-one breathing down the victim's neck to have done with it and leave the studio free for someone else.

Poor Eric Halsall and I were out of our depth, fellow fugitives from this tinsel world. The kinder everyone was to us, the more inadequate we felt. A couple of amateurs swamped by specialised professionals. If we didn't contract a near fatal inferiority complex, it was only because journalists, of necessity, are pretty pachydermatous. Used to the horse-and-buggy crews of regional television, I found a five-camera crew, of around thirty or forty strong, very intimidating. If, as sometimes happened, I made a right porridge of something and had to do it again, I was acutely aware that the rest of the crew, looking forward to getting out of the incessant Lakeland rain to relax in a snug and cosy bar parlour, must have been muttering amongst themselves about hams, up from the country, cocking things up. And, when we did get back to our hotel, my broken arm made it impossible for me to cut up my own food at table. So I had to throw myself on the mercy of my neighbour and ask him to cut each course into manageable chunks, which I could stab with my fork, as uncivilised Yankees do.

The kinder and more sympathetic everybody was, the worse I felt. The hyper-efficient wench, who initially turned me off, proved among the kindest and most helpful of them all. She turned me on again!

The most important job – to me! – of the day was to introduce each programme and wind it up, by trailing the next. This was known as 'Topping and Tailing' and was a very minor matter to the producer, who regarded it as padding to be fitted in when there was nothing urgent to do. All that really mattered was that I should be placed where the scenery behind me was out of this world, so that, if viewers were not interested in what I had to say, they would stay switched on, rivetted by the tranquillity of the view.

Having rather a long spiel to do one day, I was sent up the side of a hill, with Lake Buttermere below me and a rugged range of hills on the skyline as a backdrop. I was in the care of a stage manager who asked me to stand on the exact spot which the producer had previously selected, until he gave me my cue to speak. In front of me, between me and the lake, there was a cameraman, assistant cameraman, sound engineer and 'sparks', in case it clouded over. Our little group was

10

*The wisest dog on earth.*

several hundred yards away from the scanner, which contained the equipment and screens which were the nerve centre of the whole operation. If we had been marooned in the centre of an uninhabited desert, we could not have felt more isolated.

Eventually the stage manager gave me the signal to start spouting. A dozen words into my spiel, he drew his finger across his throat, in the conventional uncouth command to Shut Up. The producer, who was wired to converse with him through headphones, had noticed that the skyline appeared to be decapitating me. It was necessary that I stand higher, so a box was sent for, to accomplish the deception.

Five minutes later, I was perched on a box, which was below the camera's sightline. In front of me were my tiny gallery of cameraman and his satellites. The stage manager gave the sign for me to start spouting. 'Welcome,' I said, 'to this, the first ...' My masterpiece was chopped off in full flow again by the stage manager signifying my throat was cut.

11

'Sorry,' he said. 'The producer says you are still having your head chopped off by the horizon. We've got to get another box for you.' Boxes do not grow like mushrooms in the solitude of wild hills, so the second one took some time to arrive. Meanwhile, a gaggle of hikers appeared from the lower slopes and came straggling towards us.

Such woolly-hatted wanderers are pathologically curious and, seeing a group of half a dozen strangers poking out of the hillside, stark as sore thumbs in a desert, they had headed in our direction.

By this time, the second box had arrived and I clambered awkwardly on top, my broken arm, tucked into my pocket, doing nothing for my sense of balance. The delay in getting the box was putting things behind schedule, so I was bidden to get on with it.

'Welcome,' I said, 'to this, the first in a series of ...' The stage manager's throat-cutting routine halted me again.

'Not your fault,' he said. 'A cloud came over the sun and screwed the picture.' When the scenery was once more bathed in brilliance, he set me off again, but I got very little further before a low-flying plane howled over, screwing the sound.

While I was waiting for silence to return, I scrutinised the gallery of uninvited guests clustering round the cameraman, his assistant, the sound engineer and the 'sparks'. They had huge packs on their backs, boots like barges, thumb sticks and all the exaggerated paraphernalia of pantomime explorers. Swaying on my ricketty boxes, I might have been parodying Lord Soper in Hyde Park, delivering his homily to the heathens. I overheard one of them saying to his mate, 'What's he saying that for? He's already said the same thing four times.'

He had, of course, no way of knowing that innocent clouds, skylines at the wrong level, and aircraft as unwelcome as the gatecrashing hikers, had cut off my words of wisdom in full spate. The obvious mystification of my audience did nothing for my confidence, for I can conceive of nothing more calculated to make one feel more stupid than perching on two boxes, nursing a broken arm and spouting what seems like gibberish.

Eric Halsall and I were odd men out among the full-time crew. We cried on each other's shoulders in the evenings, and swapped stories of the difficulties we had been in all day. We were both agreed that we needed our heads looked at, for getting so far out of our depth, till we were invited to see some of the highlights which had been encapsulated by the camera during the day.

There were some stunning pictures of working dogs and their handlers, far better than either of us expected. Having seen the efforts of the horse-and-buggy boys in the regions, which did not compare in quality, I confided to Eric that I hadn't expected a lot of shots to come off – so I reckoned Lady Luck was an unpaid member of the crew.

The next night we saw some more shots and, at first, we thought that they had been even luckier than before. Then it dawned on us that, perhaps, it wasn't luck at all. Perhaps the outstanding quality was the product of outstanding skill?

We examined our camera-toting colleagues through fresh eyes – and they were suddenly transformed and rose-tinted. Instead of being brittle city slickers, with whom we had nothing in common, we suddenly discovered their true worth. They were real experts, whose very ability makes impossible tasks seem easy. What we had taken for luck owed nothing to chance but was consummate skill of the highest order. We suddenly realised that we were two insignificant teeth in the cogwheel of about fifty professionals, each a specialist in his own field. They were so gifted that they were always happy to give us a generous helping hand when we got into difficulties, instead of watching us flounder, as lesser men might do. Though it made us even more conscious of our own inadequacy, the task became a pleasure instead of a penance. Philip Gilbert was a purist. He had stumbled on a highly specialised minority sport and was content to introduce it to viewers exactly as it was, with no frills. The course he had laid out, on the shores of Lake Buttermere, was precisely the model of the formalised course on which shepherds tested their dogs against each other all over the British Isles.

The first test of a working sheep dog is the ability to 'gather' his sheep from a considerable distance and bring them to his master. So, at the far end of the course, a 'release' pen was constructed in which enough sheep were penned to provide a bunch of seven fresh sheep, to test the ability of every dog in the competition.

When all was ready for a trial to begin, the shepherds in charge of the release pen turned out a bunch of seven sheep and guided them gently to the starting post. When they were seen by the judges to be steady and near the starting post, the signal was given for the trial to start, and the shepherd sent his dog off to collect them, on either the right or left hand side of the course, as he chose. The judges then awarded marks for the 'outrun', or 'gather', which is the first phase of the trial, docking marks for any fault, such as running in too close and starting the sheep off in a direction other than to the shepherd.

*Sheep in the release pen. Seven are being filtered into narrow 'crush' so that they can be released for trial, without risk of more dashing out.*

The next stage in the trial is the 'lift'. Ideally, the dog should have arrived directly behind his sheep, having run in a smooth curve, towards the outside of the course, so as not to startle them. When he moves up steadily towards them, from directly behind, it is natural for them to stop grazing and move off, directly towards the shepherd. This first contact between dog and sheep is absolutely vital. A dog that bundles in too fast may startle them and make them panic away or scatter, when they will be difficult to control – apart from losing him marks.

If he is too diffident, they will immediately sense his weakness and begin to play him up. There is no creature more bloody-minded than a bloody-minded sheep. So the lift is vital in enabling good dogs to start as they mean to go on and for the sheep to appreciate if they are being shepherded by a dog which has not the strength of character to gaffer them.

14

Although dogs often have to work out of sight of the shepherd on the farm, when heather or bracken or undulating ground obscure the view, the purpose of a flat, formalised trials course is so that the spectators can see for themselves precisely how the trial is being run. People simply do not bother to go to watch such a specialised minority sport unless they comprehend the niceties. Judges themselves run their own dogs at other trials, and every regular spectator may own, or have owned, top trials dogs himself. So part of the fun is comparing your own judgement with the verdict of the judges, which would be impossible if the whole of the course was not as clearly visible to spectators as to judges.

Sheep hurdles are spaced out round the course in the form of open 'gates' – with no fence on either side of them. It is therefore perfectly easy for a sheep, or bunch of sheep, to 'miss' a gate by going round the wrong end of one of the hurdles instead of between them, a fault for which the competitor would be deducted marks. Not only must the dog drive the whole of his bunch of sheep, between gates or hurdles,

*Fitting white strip to hurdle to make it clearer to distant camera.*

15

erected in pairs, but he must also drive them from one obstacle to the next in a straight line.

Deviations from this straight and narrow path will also be penalised by loss of marks. Eric's cries of anguish, because this dog or that is 'bending', are a familiar background comment, which alerts viewers to impending catastrophe in every programme.

Enthusiasts, who know, or think they know, as much as the judges, often beg to differ. What is and what is not a bend is a matter of subjective judgement if it is not overdone. So the post mortem after every run highlights differences of opinion which spark off endless arguments among the sheep dog men who can see precisely as much of the course as the judges can.

I had my doubts about casual viewers though. The fact that this dog or that lost ten marks for bends between the fetch gates and the drive away or cross drive gates may be perfectly intelligible to countryfolk who were practically suckled between sheep hurdles, weaned on the pastures dotted among high fells, and cut their teeth on shepherds' crooks. But I felt the mystique might not get through to casual viewers before boredom set in from watching endless dogs drive sheep, times without number, round the same obstacles on a flat field.

Philip Gilbert had come to the same conclusion, so he cunningly laid out a course over which the shepherd could drive his flock from either end. This made an immense difference to the spectacle as shown upon the screen, because the views in the background were totally different. One way there was the tranquillity of Buttermere Lake. When the course was reversed, the savage, rocky heights glowered down to put things in perspective.

Not, of course, that trials, even on the most formalised courses, are restricted to the circus tricks of driving the sheep, in a set pattern, between obstacles or from one obstacle to the next.

When the sheep have proved the man and his dog's ability – or lack of it! – to fetch them from afar, bring them to the shepherd and send them where the geography of the course dictates, they are brought to the 'shedding ring'. This is a circle, ten yards or so across, marked out by small piles of sawdust, about half a bucketful apiece.

In 'singles' trials, where the shepherd works one dog, two out of each bunch of sheep have been fitted with a red leather collar, to distinguish them from their fellows. The dog drives the sheep into the shedding ring, where the shepherd meets them and halts them with

*A good shot of 'shedding' single sheep from bunch.*

When the sheep has been shed, it will try to rejoin its fellows and the dog must keep them apart until the judges cry 'that'll do', which signifies they are satisfied the dog is in command. Keeping the shed sheep away from her fellows is known as 'wearing'.

an imperious wave of his crook, making his dog lie down, on the opposite side of the sheep.

To prove their expertise, shepherd and dog are then required to separate one of the two red-collared sheep from her fellows, without any of them going over the boundary of the piles of sawdust round the shedding ring before the chosen sheep has been parted – or 'shed' from her fellows. Normally she will try to rejoin them, because sheep are flocking animals by nature and have a built-in resistance to being exposed to unknown peril on their own.

So, having accomplished the first part of the task by 'shedding' the sheep from the rest of the bunch, the dog must prevent them reuniting until the judges are satisfied that he really is in control and give the word that they are satisfied. Keeping them thus apart is known as 'wearing' them, and it is a traumatic experience for the solitary sheep so that, however gently and carefully they have been driven round the course, they are now likely to be on edge for the last stage of the trial, which is 'penning'.

A few yards from the shedding ring, a rectangular pen, of three fixed hurdles has been set up, with stakes driven in to locate them. The fourth side can be enclosed by a single hurdle, hinged at one end to the pen and attached, at the other to a length of rope nine feet long.

The shepherd holds the other end of this rope and commands his dog to drive the whole bunch of sheep into the pen. He may help by directing them with his crook, but he is not allowed to touch them with it.

When they are driven – or 'gentled' – into the pen, the man swings the gate to behind them, so ending the trial, when the number of points lost for faults can be subtracted from the starting total to give the final score.

Although the whole procedure and marking for a trial may appear to be arbitrary and complicated, it is in fact based on entirely practical lines. The dogs entered in trials, almost without exception, are genuine working dogs, who earn their keep herding sheep – and often cattle – on the farm at home. These dogs are not pampered pets, nor 'show' dogs, bred and groomed as spurious exhibits where cosmetic appearance in the show ring counts higher than doughty deeds in wild hill country. Everything that a dog is asked to do in a trial is precisely what he would have to do to earn his keep at home.

Sheep country – proper sheep country – is often in high and precipitous hills which would be impossible to farm mechanically. Grass

*Field staff erect pen.*

keep, for grazing, is often so sparse that equations to decide the viability of a farming enterprise do not calculate how many sheep can be kept to the acre, but how many acres will be needed to keep a sheep.

Once sheep are turned out in such country, there would be no means of controlling them without highly trained sheep dogs, for rocks and gradients, tree stumps and the beds of mountain streams make the terrain impassable for mechanical vehicles or farm implements invented by man. Even prohibitively expensive helicopters could not move sheep lying up in bracken, safe from flies.

Motor cycles, three-wheelers and four-wheeled 'go anywhere' vehicles powered by motor bike engines, are the latest gimmicks to be sold to those living in inaccessible hill country – but they are no more than toys to tempt those with more money than sense. They may be all right for carting odd bales of hay to places a tractor cannot reach or for farmers' sons to acquire the technique of motor cycle trials or rallies or scrambles. But as serious tools to tame previously hostile terrain they are little more than a salesman's joke.

Sheep dogs, on the other hand, can be sent out anywhere a sheep can get to round up the visible flock and winkle skulkers from deep heather or bracken, where eyes are useless to locate them but a dog will hunt them up by scent. Enormous distances often have to be covered by the dogs because, given the chance, sheep are very territorial creatures, governed, as we are, by a matriarchal society.

It would be totally uneconomic, as well as physically impractical, to surround such areas with stock-proof fencing, so that the flock is turned out onto what are often huge areas of low value land and simply driven back onto the 'home' sheep walk when the shepherd takes out his dogs to 'look' – or check – the flock.

After a time, the sheep choose and stick to their own territory, each old ewe often annexing a favourite area, over whose boundaries she does not stray. She gathers round her a social group, often her own descendants and relatives, all of which stick to the chosen territory. This is known as 'hefting', and a naturally hefted flock will stay in various social groups on the farm, without the necessity of expensive fencing to confine them.

The original hefting is done by the shepherd, who goes out daily with his dog – or sometimes lives for weeks on end in the area where he wishes his flock to reside, driving them back daily if they stray.

When properly hefted, a flock is such a valuable asset that it is sold with the land when a farm changes hands, for if it was sold to anyone within many miles it would, in any case, migrate back home by its hefting instinct.

The new owner buying the farm and its hefted flock can rely on it remaining on location for years to come, because future generations bred from the hefted ewes will themselves remain hefted to their birthland.

New blood is introduced as necessary, simply by introducing rams, or tups, of the required strains. Sex drive, not hefting instinct, prevents them straying from their ewes, till their work is done and they have sired the next generation.

Without sheep, in such inhospitable territory, the land would degenerate to bracken or gorse, or thorn or birch scrub, and become an impenetrable jungle.

Sheep can also be run on heather, which will itself degenerate if not burned, in patches, by rotation, to keep constant variety of crop. Age ranges from tall, straggly, indigestible fibre to young, succulent shoots. Burning is normally an uneconomic task, except for grouse shooting, which is a rich man's sport, able to sustain gamekeepers to manage the heather by rotational burning. The sheep also enjoy the tender young heather, recovering from previous seasons' fire, but parasitic ticks affect both species so that farmers and grouse shooters do not necessarily see eye-to-eye.

Without keepers to burn the heather, and sheep to eat the young shoots of regenerating trees, the hills would deteriorate until scrub afforestation, normally with visually unattractive softwoods, resulted.

But conservationists, dedicated to conserving what is best in our heritage, do not always realise just how much they owe to working sheep dogs, to shepherd the flocks which keep some of the wildest and most beautiful country in good heart.

By modern standards, shepherds and their dogs lead incredibly hard lives. Rain in such hill country is many times as much as rain in the eastern or southern counties. So, for days on end, both men and dogs have to work in conditions which would make urban shop stewards reach for their whistles and cry 'Everybody Out!'

Such men have no workmen's huts to creep into during every shower of rain. Merciless, shrivelling winds, which would turn lesser mortals' guts to water, are shrugged off with the understatement 'fresh'.

Loneliness is their norm, for they work, for days on end, in wild solitudes where the only company is the sheep and their dogs, which are the tools of their trade as well as their bosom companions.

When heavy snow drifts and buries the sheep, it is the dog which locates them, by scent and faint whispers of sound, so that the shepherd knows precisely where to dig to rescue them. When hill mists thicken to impenetrable fog, it is the dog whose instinct pilots his master home to the farmstead. If, as sometimes happens, the shepherd slips on treacherous rocks, injuring himself too badly to struggle home, he sends the dog back as the pilot for friends or family to come out to rescue him.

Viewers, watching the apparently casual relationship between man and dog, can be totally deceived about the real intensity and depth of the partnership. After a championship triumph, which may put both man and dog on a pinnacle of their profession, there is none of the pretentious ostentation of prizewinners at minor dog shows, who punch the air and hug their pooches and mouth spurious sympathy over defeated rivals.

Shepherds take the smooth with the rough. They may give the dog a cursory pat, but the height of the praise they will lavish will be a curt 'That'll do'. Then they stride off the field as if such coveted prizes are an everyday occurrence.

Such undemonstrative lack of emotion is really the facade which cloaks the modesty of the nicest people. The truth is that they are intensely proud of their dogs and love basking in the reflected glory of a dog which brings them fame by winning a major event.

Just as the most delightful people I know all like nice dogs, so all real dog-men believe that their dog, warts and all, is the best dog in the world, and they have an insatiable urge to prove the point by beating their mates in open competition.

They work together all day, knowing each other's faults, so the cleverest shepherds are constantly trying to mitigate any small deficiency in his dog's performance and to improve their teamwork. There comes a time when the dog is ready to be entered in minor – or 'nursery' – trials to gain experience of working strange sheep near strange dogs, and ignoring the distractions inseparable from spectators.

Working a dog before critical and knowledgeable fellow professionals gets the adrenalin running in any red-blooded countryman, however impassive his outer shell may seem to the onlookers. His tension is transmitted to his dog and their teamwork is exciting both to watch and analyse. The urge to compete is as addictive as hard drugs.

The result is encapsulated, we hope, with the minimum of fuss and hype, in the programme *One Man and His Dog*.

Eric and I soon learned that, however hard a producer tries to give a real picture of such simple rural sport, those on the spot are painfully aware how deceptive appearances can be.

When I damaged a leg three weeks before one series, I could not drive a car, and the BBC had to send a driver to collect me. I told my surgeon, who had been treating the swelling, that I simply must be able to get a wellie boot on by the next week because it was always wet in the Lake District. I pointed out that I should look stupid in carpet slippers – the only footwear I could get on – when everyone else was booted for the weather.

'You'll be all right,' he said. 'You have nothing to do but wander round, chatting up a few old farmers. I wish my job was as easy as yours.' When his receptionist gave me the bill for this advice, I wished my job was as profitable as his!

Many viewers are under the same delusion. They see Eric and me, chatting to competitors or judges to a backdrop of the most marvellous scenery in the world, for autumn in deep English countryside is unmatchable elsewhere.

All they see is this couple of old jossers, apparently alone in the wild country with a handful of rustic men and their dogs. If the camera disclosed what lay behind and around us, they would certainly be in for a shock.

Concealed in a fold of the hills, or screened by convenient woodland, there is a complex of trucks to rival a circus encampment. The largest vehicle is the huge scanner van, which is thirty-six feet long and weighs nineteen tons. It is eight feet two inches wide – the last two inches occasionally determining the possibility of using the chosen site, for the lanes leading to such isolated spots are often critically narrow. They are also tortuous, especially those which snake their way up hairpin bends into the hills, for the 'rolling English drunkards

*Steve Morris, director, in the scanner. Each of seven cameras is connected to one of the small monitors so that Steve can see precisely what is in focus for each camera. He can give directions to come in closer or otherwise alter the shot until he is entirely satisfied, when he only has to press a button on the keyboard in front of him to transfer the shot to the large master screen below the 'no smoking' sign, when it will be recorded on the master tape. Meanwhile he is giving instructions to the other cameramen round the course to get the exact shot or cut-away shot he requires to go next on the master tape. This eventually produces a complete record of the whole run which can be edited, in due course, by Ian Smith when he returns to London.*

who made the winding English roads' did not have gigantic scanners in mind when they surveyed the routes from horseback.

Nor can the men who built little brick bridges over gurgling streams have imagined that the bridges might be expected to carry nineteen-ton loads, when the heaviest burden a team of three horses could pull was little more than a tenth of that weight.

The scanner is the nerve centre of operations. Eric and I quip that it is only there to keep the producer or director dry and sweet-tempered, while we are getting wet – but the gaffers think otherwise. Above a desk is a battery of seven small monitors, like small domestic television sets, each connected by cable to a camera, cunningly sited and camou-flaged as a pigeon shooter, at a vantage point out on the trials field. It had to be concealed with the greatest care so as to avoid startling the sheep, adding incalculable hazards for the dog driving them. It was equally vital that no camera was in the field of view of another camera, because the impression that viewers are the unseen eavesdroppers on a rural ritual in a beautiful and isolated place is an important part of the producer's task. Near the scanner is a generator capable of powering the whole galaxy of ancillary equipment, with cables disappearing in every direction. They are laid in position by a gang of 'riggers', who have the roughest physical job of the whole crew for,

*The mess tent.*

in wet weather, every joint has to be so watertight that the bitterest driving rain cannot seep through, or a vital camera might be put out of action at a critical – and unrepeatable – moment which could decide the winner of the championship.

The first job every morning is for the engineers and riggers to check every joint in the cable network – and put it right if overnight rain has done its worst. As well as this obviously vital sophisticated equipment, there is a mess tent, where lunch and tea (and mid-morning coffee!) is dispensed to competitors and crew, and a portable loo, to dispose of the surplus with propriety.

As a result, however rurally isolated Eric and I may seem to be, viewers able to cover the whole scene, instead of only the competitors' arena, would be astonished to find such a hive of activity, with equipment alone worth in excess of one and a quarter million pounds.

The money conscious might wonder how it is possible to justify the use of such a large crew, with astronomically expensive equipment, to show a few shepherds at the back of beyond, chasing sheep round an obstacle-strewn course with their dogs, however well trained to circus pitch. It would, indeed, be totally uneconomic to take such a large crew and so much equipment hundreds of miles to record a single programme, and to return each week to record another programme in the series. By keeping crew and necessary competitors on site, till the whole task is accomplished, the cost slumps.

So the gear is all assembled on site and, as Mahommet went to the mountain, the shepherds gather round the gear, so that the whole series can be recorded during the inside of a single week.

It sounds all right, if you say it quickly, but the fact is that it is an extremely high rate of production by any television standards.

Hotels and digs for the whole crew are booked for a week, and the gear all arrives on site over the weekend before the trials.

The producer, with Eric and some of his chums from the local sheep dog world, mark out the course to the pattern decided when the site was originally selected. On Monday morning, the owner of the sheep, hired for the competition, drives a few around the course, to check that there are no unforeseen snags.

By lunchtime, the cameras are all in position, cabled back to the nerve centre in the scanner, so another bunch of sheep are taken round, probably several times, after lunch, to check that the cameras can 'see' every inch of the action and that the background scenery makes a telegenic scene as perfect as is humanly possible.

*An elevated camera.*

The competitors arrive on Tuesday morning and a bunch of sheep is taken round the course once more, partly so that they can see precisely where they will be required to guide them, but also so that they can assess the natural hazards and will have a reasonable chance of forestalling disaster.

Each country fields three representatives so that, on each of the first four days, one country settles its own National Television Champion, who then goes on to meet one of the other National Champions in the semi-final.

At the semi-final stage, the first of two rounds of the Brace Championship is run, when each competitor works two dogs at the same time.

This is by no means the circus trick that it may sound. Like singles trials, the brace is a really practical test of a dog's ability on the farm. The areas where a flock may roam, when grazing is sparse, are truly prodigious, and much of the hillside may be blanketed with bracken or gorse, in which the sheep may hide. One lone dog would stand small chance of bringing down the whole flock of several hundred, under such circumstances, so several dogs are often worked at the same time.

Each dog must work to its own individual whistle or voice commands, so that, for example, one dog can be stationed to forestall escape along a difficult gully, while one or more other dogs are dispatched to distant parts of the hill to round up and concentrate scattered animals. Without such canine teamwork, hundreds of thousands of acres of potentially profitable sheep walks would be totally unfarmable and would revert to scrub or be afforested.

A practical way of testing the ability of good dogs to work together is to run two of them, as a team, round a formalised 'brace' course in a Sheep Dog Trial.

The actual recording of the first programme of each series, comprising three trials to settle one National Champion is completed on Tuesday afternoon.

The second and third programmes are completed on Wednesday, the fourth and fifth on Thursday, the sixth and seventh on Friday, and the Final by lunchtime on Saturday. Sunday is reserved in case hill mist or other catastrophe of weather makes one day impossible, or because of mechanical breakdown.

The extra day has only been needed once, when the main generator, powering the whole unit, packed up, and a replacement had to be brought in, overnight, from a hundred miles or so away.

So, however costly a crew of forty to fifty technicians and all their equipment may sound, the productivity is so high that each programme works out extremely cheaply.

The crew copes because they are hand-picked and highly professional.

Eric and I were not chosen for that first series though because of our technical television competence. Eric was picked because he had forgotten more about sheep and sheep dogs than most people would ever know, so could cope with commentaries and give much-needed advice if there were technical problems with the sheep on course, or if the competitors were not happy with the way things were going. I was picked because I had been involved with a lot of rural and 'doggy' programmes, albeit at the more leisurely pace of one-horse Regional Television.

Most of Eric's work is commentary, laid on out of vision in the studio, after the recording has been edited, so there was no great worry about his performance, since, however uncomfortable for him, he could be required to do the commentary over and over again, if necessary, until the producer was satisfied it was acceptable. My

27

'topping and tailing', when I introduced a programme directly to camera, could also, in theory, be done several times if I made a porridge of them first time.

In my case, however, I was uncomfortably aware that I would be keeping the whole crew of forty or fifty highly skilled – and pretty hard-boiled! – professionals hanging around, and, having heard their comments about other presenters who were less than competent, I had every incentive to get it right first time and try to earn the nickname One-Take Drabble!

They turned out to be a delightful bunch, who put down any fluffs to discomfort of my broken arm, but I heaved a sigh of relief when the end of the week came, all the same.

When we started the week, Eric and I decided they were far too urbanised and slick for our taste. By Saturday we were conscious of our luck in landing with such delightful professionals, with whom it was a great privilege to work. They made the impossible look easy, and not only tolerated two who were but raw novices by comparison, but went out of their way to make us feel at home. Even the producer's high-stepping dolly bird turned out to be charmingly human, with a reassuring knack of forestalling any avoidable catastrophe. She was an integral part of a creative team. We wouldn't have missed it for the world.

# 2
# Change Partners

WE RAN THE first series at Buttermere, and the second at Loweswater, which was equally dramatic scenery. It was then decided to get away from the Lake District and we went to Austwick, in North Yorkshire, which was dour, forbidding country, with grey stone walls, topped by what appeared to be an unwashed blanket of threatening dark clouds. At the end of the series, it was announced that Philip Gilbert, the producer, was being moved to 'administrative' work – where his undoubted skills as a producer would be forever stifled.

The programme was dropped the next year and, in a way, Eric and I were relieved. Viewer figures for the first three had been high for BBC-2, netting an estimated two million or so viewers. 'Appreciation' figures had been even higher, sometimes reaching eighty per cent.

These figures are obtained by trained market researchers, who use a panel of viewers, theoretically chosen to give an accurate representative cross-section, according to social status, age, and all the other factors which are supposed to comprise the strata of our society. These people are asked to view specific chosen programmes, stating how much they like them against a scale of one hundred. They are not only asked what they liked, and why, but for detailed reactions to contributors taking part and the performance of professional presenters and commentators.

Although we did not record a new series the season Philip Gilbert was moved on, a repeat of the last series was shown. It continued to figure very high in the ratings, so the Powers-that-Be decreed that the programme should be continued, with another producer.

Eric and I were not so sure. My initial misgivings were contagious

29

and had shaken Eric's confidence too. I still felt that the thrills of watching one man, however charming, blowing a whistle while his dog chased a bunch of sheep round a formalised course, might soon wear thin.

Add to that the fact that we would be working for a strange producer, who would want to be different but might not be better, and the project no longer seemed a commercial risk. We felt that we might be wiser to fade gracefully away, while the programme was still on top of the world, than to go down with what could so easily be a sinking ship.

I feared it might not last because it was still being portrayed as the purist, specialised sport of a highly trained dog, a bunch of sheep to be driven through obstacles on a course as predictable as moves on a chess board. To appreciate the spectacle to the full, it was vital to understand the detailed why's and wherefores of every command. Newcomers, watching for the first time, might soon regard it as repetitious and switch over to the inevitable smart-Alec knocking the Establishment. The novelty, which had sparked off such satisfactory viewing figures, could soon wear off, and it seemed better to call it a day. We could be duly grateful for being invited to take part in a programme which might be remembered with affection.

We all met up at Chatsworth, where the Supreme International was being run by the International Sheep Dog Society, the governing body of the sheep dog world.

The Supreme International, which sorts out the champion of champions in England, Scotland, Ireland and Wales, is the Blue Riband for which real sheep dog handlers would give their souls, and everybody who is anybody in sheep dog circles can be found at the 'Supreme', among spectators, competitors, or judges.

Ian Smith, who was to be the producer of future *One Man and His Dog* series, was introduced to us by Philip Gilbert, who was just bowing out.

We were all a bit stiff-legged. Eric, who revolves at the centre of a world of sheep and sheep dogs, felt that this newcomer knew even less than Philip Gilbert. Nothing must be done to sully the purity of traditional trialling. My worries were very different. I had done my homework and discovered that Ian Smith was a very distinguished producer of 'Outside Broadcasts', used to dealing with professionals of the highest calibre, on programmes such as Superstars and the BAFTA Academy Awards programmes. He now produces Trooping the Colour and the Remembrance Day Service as well as *One Man and His Dog*.

*Monarch of all he surveys, Ian Smith, producer.*

His presenters were national figures, slick, sleek and unflappable. I had no illusions that I was in the same league, since my experience had been mainly with fellow country men, in relaxed and spontaneous conversation. Although Ian was obviously a kind and cheerful soul, it was unlikely that he had got to the top of his tough profession without pretty steely fingers encased within his velvet gloves! Presenters in his line of business are highly expendable – and I have always believed in getting out before I am pushed when exits are inevitable.

I had been wrong in my initial assessment, when I gave tongue that the idea was too repetitive to work, though I still believe that, if we had continued to expect viewers to be satisfied indefinitely with anything so specialised, the figures would inevitably have sagged into decline.

Ian had similar views. He wouldn't have accepted the assignment himself if he didn't think he could make it work, because, like contributors, producers are also rated only as good as their last programme. Television is a ruthless world, where little fleas are forever queuing up to climb on the backs of big fleas who have gone over the top. Looking at the programme with completely fresh eyes, Ian had come to the conclusion that the real potential in showing shepherds and their dogs was not to delight a miniscule audience, already besotted by their purist games of canine chess. He realised that trialling was really only the stage on which to show the everyday skills of dogs, who earned their living in solitudes of remote hill country, where they were never seen except by the men who worked the dogs.

So what he intended to do was to modify the formalised course on which trials are normally run, so that it contained the precise hazards and difficulties which shepherds and dogs faced in their everyday work.

Dyed-in-the-wool enthusiasts – including Eric – liked a course where every inch was visible to spectators, who were usually as knowledgeable as the official judges. This was 'fair' to competitors, who could see every move of dog and sheep and forestall disaster by shrill blasts on their whistles, at the first sign that things were not under control.

It was equally agreeable to specialist spectators, who could see for themselves the good and bad points in every run, and hold endless post mortems on the strength – and weakness! – of the judges' verdicts when the winner was announced.

But to casual viewers, each run was often so like the last that separating wheat from chaff and appreciating finer technicalities could be more like mental work than entertainment.

Ian Smith proposed to run his television trials over a course with many of the features which might be found in the hills where sheep are shepherded commercially.

When a shepherd has to collect his flock for shearing or dipping or worming, there are always sheep hidden from view behind rocks, in gullies, or buried from sight in heather or bracken. The dog has to use eyes and nose and ears and, above all, initiative to winkle them into view before the shepherd can give his whistle-coded commands to guide them this way or that, to find the easiest route down.

Provided that this is explained to viewers, Ian's belief was that the spectacle would enthral vast numbers of previously disinterested urban spectators as much as more knowledgeable rustics.

Eric was initially horrified. He thought the competitors might mutiny if asked to drive sheep in competition over a course they could not supervise adequately. The fact that spectators might witness errors competitors had no chance of correcting – because they could not see them – simply added injury to insult.

Ian's view was that, if we wished to increase momentum – or even maintain our position in the ratings – it was vital to widen the attraction, to bring in viewers who might never be gripped by the finer points of maintaining straight lines between obstacles or going too wide on the outrun. He felt that the spectacle of seeing how the other half lived would fascinate city dwellers, who were tied to office chairs for five days a week, and fugitives from the urban ratrace for the other two days. A trials course, he felt, which was laid out to give the flavour of real shepherding in wild sheep country, would attract more viewers than what casual observers might take for a bit of a circus act.

A few intellectual trendies still whinge that 'turning sheep dog trials into "entertainment" destroys their integrity.' The opposing school holds the view that anything which sharpens the urban minority's appreciation and understanding of rural life can only do good.

I belong to the latter school, I see nothing wrong in turning sheep dog trials into entertainment if that persuades more commuters and city dwellers, who might not be able to distinguish a bull from a bulrush in the field, to enjoy and understand rural crafts and pastimes, which they knew nothing about until they appeared on the box in their sitting room.

The technological revolution has created change on such a scale that there is a massive sense of insecurity because none of us know what tomorrow may bring. This has sired deep nostalgia for 'simple' things. Anything ancient, which has deep roots in the past, is suddenly important. Surviving antiquity holds out hope for the future. Folklore and traditional crafts have become suddenly fashionable. Organic foods, undefiled by scientists, are no longer old-hat but marketable products, more tasty and healthy than supermarket junk.

Sheep dog trialling meets all these criteria. Dogs are man's best friends, the very emblems of fidelity. Herding dogs which win trials today could be bred from the same stock which were the partners of our ancestors, when they were first transformed from hunters to primitive farmers and stock breeders. Watching the mental affinity between a shepherd and his dog, it needs little imagination to transpose them both back thousands of years into the past.

Far more important, is the vision of sheep dogs still herding sheep in the hills in time as far ahead as they did in the past. Such faith in the future, inspired by one man and his best friend, is very comforting.

Clever boffins have invented sophisticated machines which have changed the face of the countryside more in our generation than it has changed for centuries. But most of the disruption has been in the lowlands, where hedges have been bulldozed out, to make prairies of plough. Subsidies have made it economic to fill in small pools, where soil is deep and fertile, so that the spaces they occupied, like oases in a desert, can be ploughed to enrich the rest of the bare soil. Huge trees can now be snatched out by the roots, as vandals pluck flowers in inner cities. Machines are becoming our masters instead of our slaves.

But it is still uneconomic to squander hard cash on juggernauts in the sort of hill country which is ideal for sheep. The soil is too poverty stricken to grow crops and, in any case, the stone is often so near the surface that the most expensive brain children of inventors would make no fortunes for their owners because it takes several acres to grow enough keep to feed a single sheep.

There are literally hundreds of thousands of acres of such hill country which will keep sheep or grouse or deer – but nothing else. If some maniac accountant, farming from a city-based computer, is ever fool enough to rig the price of lamb and mutton so that it becomes uneconomic to farm sheep in the hills, he will put those hundreds of thousands of acres in mortal peril.

Left to itself, without sheep to graze off emergent hawthorn and bramble and birch, the hilly landscape would degenerate to worthless scrub. The only way to control that – apart from hardy sheep to bite it off – would be to plant forests of sterile foreign pines, which already

34

*The field staff, who bring the sheep to the release pen, release the right number for each trial (seven for singles trials, and young handlers, and eight for brace trials). They move them to the exhaust pen when they have been penned, fit coloured (red) collars as necessary, erect the gates and pens as requested and are generally indispensable.*

elicit screeches of complaint from lovers of aesthetic countryside.

So long as agricultural sanity reigns, there should be no danger of that, and sheep should monopolise the hills as far into the future as they have in the past.

They cannot do so without skilled shepherds and wise dogs, for neither helicopters nor motor bikes could find them, under cover, nor negotiate the rocks and gullies and shifting scree where they can scrape a living.

So our sheep dog trials not only give the flavour of a past, which has not changed for millennia, but a glimpse into the future as well. They provide a rare promise that the simple life, for which so many crave, is not an unattainable dream. So I believed that Ian Smith's proposal to highlight more general rural facets was eminently practical. He calculated he would attract a wider audience than specialists who could appreciate the finer points of the judges' marking. The proof has been that the programme has rolled on from strength to strength, and is now nationally known and held in high affection.

Spreading the net so wide made things difficult for Eric, though. His commentary has to dot the 'i's' and cross the 't's' for townsfolk who have never seen a sheep dog trial and know nothing about training dogs or the reasons for erecting bogus 'gates' in the middle of the landscape, with no fence near them so that the sheep can as easily go round as through them, but are penalised if they do.

Anyone who has ever kept – and driven! – sheep will be painfully aware that, to mix a metaphor, they are among the most pig-headed, bloody-minded brutes in God's creation. It is hard enough to persuade a bunch of them to go through a gap in a fence without scattering. To get them all between two hurdles, stuck up like sore thumbs in a desert, is infinitely harder. Novice man or dogs would lose them over the horizon.

All that, plus the fact that they are supposed to keep in a straight line from obstacle to obstacle, has to be explained, in simple terms, to viewers who have not watched a trial before.

But, as soon as they have grasped such essentials, they feel as well informed as seasoned addicts and write in to say 'What's he telling us that for? We know about the course. Get your commentator to shut up a bit.'

If poor Eric does shut up, newcomers complain that it is all Greek to them, and switch over to another channel. So Eric has to walk a perpetual tightrope, forever striving to be informative over the finer points while avoiding repetition wherever he can.

Ian is such a past master of his profession that he minimises such problems by deliberately widening the scope of the programme. Far from being a theoretical purist, he now produces a programme which is not just about sheep dog trialling. It is a country magazine programme with shepherds and their dogs as focal points.

I have met and talked with shepherds and dry stone wallers, who have recalled centuries long gone, in the Cotswolds, where the wool trade was once so popular that great churches were built, on the spoils from golden fleeces, as status symbols for rich merchants who made their fortunes there.

Gordon Beningfield, an eminent rural artist and a personal friend of mine, has shared with us the antique treasures he has amassed in his collection of shepherds' bygones.

36

We have filmed at sheep fairs and watched ewes giving birth to their lambs, and learned the secrets of a bell wether, which was the castrated leader of the flock. Sheep fairs and shepherds' huts and the stone effigy of Tiddles, the church cat sleeping till eternity in the churchyard, are no longer mysteries to regular viewers of the programme. Stately homes and humble cottages have both provided hospitality to all enthralled by sheep dog trials. Perhaps the most popular feature of all the items we have shown have been concerned with the art of making shepherds' crooks, where traditional craftsmanship merges with pure art.

Before persuading viewers to settle down to such a wide-ranging rural magazine, it is vital to get them hooked, so Ian Smith's first priority is to choose a site with scenery so stunning that viewers simply cannot turn away.

Most of us have some favourite secret spot to which we return for solace when pressures get us down, so that it was not too difficult to choose the first few sites. But, having found scenery which is generally acknowledged to be out of this world, it becomes progressively more difficult to 'top' it for the next series.

Competitors themselves are an obviously rich source of inspiration, for they spend their working lives in precisely the sort of country where city-bound folk would spend their holidays – if only they knew of its existence.

*Tiddles the church cat rests in Fairford churchyard near the tombstones of the wool merchants who grew prosperous off the backs of sheep. Tiddles kept the sacred precincts free from mice from 1963 to 1980.*

37

There are all sorts of snags when suggestions are asked for, though! The most beautiful spot in England – or Scotland or Wales – may turn out to be totally inaccessible to cars, far less to the heavy equipment such as scanner vans. Or the site may be on an aeroplane flight path, which would submerge the visual tranquility in an intolerable bedlam of raucous noise. Not only do we need a perfect backcloth, as varied as possible for different camera shots, it is just as essential to have large enough space to contain the trials course.

Ian, who has an artist's eye for the composition of a picture, loves a mountain stream, cascading over rocks, or a placid lake or telegenic river, because water, especially moving water of limpid purity, provides a focus of sheer pleasure to fill occasional, inevitable gaps in the action.

Such site selection is so important that the producer is prepared to spend days on end in search of the ideal.

The first priority is to decide the general location. We spread sites around England and Scotland and Wales fairly evenly for the simple, pragmatic reason that both competitors and viewers would feel hard-done-to if 'their' native heath did not get a fair share of the limelight and nobody would deny that all three countries contain scenery as good as – or better than – any fashionable foreign land.

So of course does Ireland – and we would love to go there – but the programme has to run on a very tight financial budget and the sheer cost of transporting forty or fifty technicians, with cars and technical equipment, overseas would bust the bank before we started.

Having decided in which country to hold his trials 'this' year, Ian has to do a cold appraisal of the terrain of recent programmes. Scenery has often been so superb that it has seemed impossible to better it, and the obvious alternative has been to choose somewhere so different that there is no yardstick by which to measure the relative attractions, as apples cannot be qualified against oranges.

Such a routine narrows the choice down to manageable proportions. After a couple of series in dramatic lakeland scenery, it may be decided to go to a great estate, like Chatsworth, since farmers keep sheep in the more fertile lowlands or downlands as well as in hill country. Or to a Welsh estate, such as Rhiewlas, at Bala, in North Wales, where the first sheep dog trial had been organized by Squire Lloyd-Price, a century earlier, in 1878, and where his descendant still lives.

But it is easy to run out of steam by relying on personal preference for favourite spots or historic associations, such as the centenary of the first recorded trial. A more obvious way is to ask the shepherds themselves, because shepherding their flock obviously takes them into secluded wildernesses which casual visitors would never stumble into if they wandered for a lifetime.

Sometimes, of course, shy countrymen are too modest to claim that their 'own' private spot is better than anyone else's. Or they do not wish to share the secret. So they suggest some other attractive site on the land of a neighbour, who may well be flattered and welcome us with open arms.

With all the predictable snags in mind, Ian sees as many 'possibles' as he can, assesses them as potential breath-stoppers and makes a shortlist. Then he goes again, with Eric, who assesses the shortlist to confirm that it is possible to lay out a course there which would be a fair and acceptable test for working sheep dogs and the men who partner them.

Coming to a final decision from such a choice is obviously time consuming and, like being asked to draw the winning ticket for a raffle from the hat, it tends to leave the owner of the chosen spot delighted and the rest of the shortlist less than pleased. Each is convinced that his choice is head and shoulders best so that the chosen alternative course must have been decided by favouritism or worse!

Imagine the feeling of poor Ian, when the final section is irreversible, if he looks over the brow of the hill to a neighbour's land, only to discover an incomparably better spot, when it is too late to change his mind and flit to the rainbow's end.

A fringe benefit of earning my living by writing and broadcasting about the countryside is that I travel widely. I am privileged to work on great estates and see behind the scenes where casual visitors could not intrude.

Great estates, which have been in the same family for many generations often have a marvellous relationship between owners and tenants and staff which would be the envy of the best run commercial enterprises.

Having spent a considerable time, over the years, working at Chatsworth, the home of the Duke and Duchess of Devonshire, I have got to know both the owners and others who live on their estate on a free and easy basis – and I have yet to hear a snide remark or unfriendly word for the simple reason that there are no sides. They are all pulling in the same direction.

I found precisely the same during the twenty odd years I spent in industry. Family firms, small enough for the boss to know every employee and often to be able to do his job as well or better than he could, had a close enough relationship for everyone to appreciate that, if the firm didn't do well, they would all be out of a job. It became 'our' firm and there was a genuine team spirit. But growth sometimes made them victims of their own success because strangers and 'experts' were brought in who had no personal loyalty and, once the notion was floated that it was only 'their' money, instead of 'ours' that was being spent security vanished out of the window. Such loyalties have ensured the continuity and character of ancient lines of great landowners who, in turn, have created the infinite variety which sets the English countryside so far above the most exotic foreign rivals.

Death duties and the occasional degenerate, insipid owners have resulted in the break-up of many great estates which have fallen into the hands of the National Trust to be kept in trust for the benefit of the nation.

I have seen a good many such cases because the wild country, which is the natural home of sheep dog trialling, hound trailing and gatherings such as Appleby Fair, is often difficult to manage profitably so that the taxman acts as executioner of the traditional rights of ownership.

The National Trust is now among our largest, if not greatest land-owners because, being an official trust, it is not subject to the crippling taxes levied on the real owners.

By the same token, it is so large that it is as impersonal as huge industrial conglomerates and tenants of the Trust seem to be regarded as impersonal pawns in the bureaucratic paperwork, as unimportant as factory staff who appear only as figures on a balance sheet.

Wherever I go, in such wild and beautiful places, bitter tenants tell similar stories. The buzz word, in agriculture, is 'diversification' because it grows harder to earn a living as chemical farming and intensive methods have produced mountains of surplus, where supply has exceeded demand. Accountant boffins, in the Common Market, are under the delusion that the basic laws of supply and demand can be overridden by juggling with figures, which are making the capital-intensive farmers richer and sheep farmers, trying to wrest a living in wild – and beautiful – hill country poorer to the point of extinction.

But, if they try to diversify, by using tourism as a crop and converting buildings for visitors or setting up camping or caravan sites, their landlords, the National Trust, step in and block the scheme. They point out that the lease is for *farming* activities, taking the bureaucratic view

40

that the countryside can be frozen, as it is, rather than allowed to shift to the pressures of inevitable change.

But it is impossible to stop the clock and changes in wild country are as inevitable as lowland changes which have resulted, over the centuries, in continuous woodland being broken up to allow villages and farms to be carved out which are now giving way to ever larger fields to accommodate the immense scale of modern machinery.

Few hill tenants of the Trust have a good word for their landlords and I have even met men who say they have been forbidden to accept financial recompense for the disturbance caused by television crews and equipment on their land 'because such payments are not included in the terms of their lease!'

Such a pennywise policy is likely to prove pound foolish because the publicity for their cause accruing from exposure on the box, together with genuine appreciation for the job they do could have resulted in additional members!

Choosing a site with a view is only the beginning. The next stage is to make a physical check to be sure that everything that matters can really get there. The longest and heaviest vehicle is the scanner and enquiries have to be made to ensure that every little bridge will carry it without collapsing. When the theoretical limit of safe load over little bridges is critically close to the weight of the scanner, it may also be necessary to assess the physical condition of the bridge as well as the weight for which it was designed.

After loads have been checked, widths come into their own importance, because roads and gateways designed in the spacious days of horse and cart did not cater for such juggernauts. Nor did the chaps who cut hairpin bends on the sides of mountains, dream that vehicles more than half the length of a cricket pitch would ever try to snake their way round them. Finally, when the relatively(!) sound surface of public roads degenerates into farm tracks, it is vital to find out if the farmer minds what may be the access to his farmstead for the daily milk lorry, being temporarily mutilated. And, if he is prepared to shrug that off, how far or how difficult it will be to import stone to repair it, when we have done, because we naturally wish to leave it as good or better than we found it.

Arrangements have to be made for an on-site caterer who will supply the whole crew and competitors with a drink at morning coffee break, a substantial hot lunch, and tea and biscuits some time in the afternoon.

Ian Smith is of the persuasion which believes an army marches on its stomach, and he always arranges for a mess tent large enough to seat everyone in comfort – except when it occasionally blows down! Small firms usually do the catering and they make a splendid job of it, without any fancy frills. The fare is plain but plentiful, because after half a day exposed to all the Weatherman on the Wireless failed to predict, appetites are at least as sharp as campers'. Some measure of the mutual satisfaction Ian Smith engenders can be gleaned from the fact that the same caterer appeared, year after year, at sites hundreds of miles apart. He continued to come 'as a holiday job' long after he had ditched less congenial assignments, and finally stopped only when the economics of complete retirement forced him to sell his redundant van and equipment. A huge Portaloo completes the gear necessary to cater for our basic needs.

Spectators could be one of the great problems. Conventional sheep dog trials, where the tiny crowd are as knowledgeable as competitors and judges, attract only purists, who are likely to know almost every-one there by sight, if not personally. The chances are that many of them have met before, in competition – or have possibly sat on the rostrum, in judgement of each other's performance. Only their current dogs decide which role they play, because it is their performance, with a dog as partner, which decides whether they are picked to compete for their country, in International Trials, or whether they are scrapping it out far down the hierarchy, for a place in a top grade team. Since only a handful of really star handlers are lucky (or skilful!) enough to get more than two or three equally brilliant dogs in a lifetime, there are always more who know how the job is done than are currently demonstrating the skill themselves.

For that reason, regular spectators are never a problem. Their own grapevine tells them where our next series will be run, and if they turn up to watch, they are as welcome as the actual families of the competitors. What is more, they always look 'right' when the camera picks them out in the background, because countrymen seem to know instinctively how to dress for such occasions. Townsfolk, on holiday, tend to ponce themselves up in 'casual' gear consisting of blue denims, like mechanic's overalls, topped off with woolly hats and gaudy anoraks, which are obtrusive among the soft shades of hill or lakeland scenery.

*Spectators at the foot of Ian's tower. A camera is sited on top.*

Countryfolk, on the other hand, always seem neat and respectable when attending country fairs or shows or competitive events like sheep dog trials. They leave their working clothes – which may be denim but are not gaudy! – at home, and turn up in a jacket and trousers, which would not be out of place if they were invited for Sunday lunch. Many of the competitors and judges wear tweed suits and either leather boots or wellingtons, depending on the weather. A large influx of urban outsiders in such a homely crowd would appear as out of place as shirts without ties at the opera.

So the venue for recording the next series is not publicised. This does not mean that strangers are not welcome, but simply that viewers who take the trouble to write to the producer to enquire where we shall be are preferred. The chances are that, if they are that keen, they will merge happily with the regulars and get mutual pleasure from each other's company. Over the years we have noticed that spectators who take the trouble to discover the next location arrive to meet what we all regard as old friends. The other great advantage, of course, is that everyone in the crew is so busy doing his own specific job that there simply would not be time to marshal crowds to avoid them intruding between hidden cameramen and their subjects. 'Regular' spectators are soon proud that they know enough to wear a cloak of invisibility without prompting by a non-existent marshal.

Some of these possibilities will appear better than others 'on camera' and, much as we would like one side or the other favoured, to optimise the background and scenery, it is out of our control so that the cameras may have to be moved slightly to get the best of all worlds.

A bone of contention between those who claim there should be no changes in such a purist, ritualistic sport and those who believe that it should interest and delight as many viewers as possible, is the sheer length of each run. In major National and International trials, the course is longer than ours, with the same number of obstacles, in the form of 'gates' sheep have to be driven through, but greater distances between them than we like.

There is a very good reason for this. In a programme forty-five minutes long, we normally show three trials, of seven or eight minutes each, using the rest of the programme for various rural 'magazine' items, such as exhibitions of shepherds' crooks, crook-making, or visits to delightful characters connected with sheep or sheep dogs.

So Ian Smith not only chose courses which were more 'natural' and picturesque than more clinically formal courses, but he deliberately

44

foreshortened them as well. He aimed to show all the normal obstacles, so that the dog had to bring his packet of sheep through the fetch gates and the cross-drive and drive-away gates, into the shedding ring, to finish with the 'pen'.

The fact that the course had been foreshortened slightly reduced the time taken to negotiate it nearer to the seven or eight minutes allocated for it in the programme – but even so, the actual time depended on the shepherd, his dog, and, not least, how stroppy or obliging the particular bunch of sheep were.

If some real crisis developed and a sheep bolted from her fellows or broke out of the pen, or, as very often happens, flatly refused to be separated from her fellows in the shedding ring, the trial could extend to a quarter of an hour or so. However long it took, the final record had to be edited down to the allowed time in the studio, weeks or sometimes months after the original had been recorded.

If five or so minutes have got to come out, to avoid the programme overrunnning, it is obvious that the object will be to remove the least interesting part of the tape, leaving all the critical highlights in. This is far more difficult than it may sound.

The complete record is sent back to London for the individual episodes to be edited, together with the magazine items, made separately, into a coherent whole of the *precise* length for which the programme is planned.

The decision about which incidents to leave in and which must be cut is obviously subjective and the success or failure of the whole programme depends on this construction.

It might be tempting to remove 'dull' shots, without apparent incident, where the victorious dog happened to have piled up his winning points, and to leave in the exciting crisis shots, where everything seemed to be going wrong. The reverse might happen with the losing dog, if his faults happened to be unspectacular and his successes had been visually exciting.

The upshot could so easily be, when several minutes had been axed from the run of each dog, that the programme, seen by viewers, would make nonsense of the result, making the genuine winner seem to have no logical reason to portray his victory and the loser look unlucky, since his faults lay on the cutting room floor. There is a most ingenious way of avoiding such a catastrophe.

Before each trial, Eric starts with a plan of the course, from starting post to pen. Marks are not awarded with points for good moves. They are deducted from the possible maximum for faults, so that, by sitting with the judges, it is possible to mark on the plan the exact places where each dog was penalised, with the number of marks – or degree of fault – entered alongside. Against each lot of marks deducted, Eric writes in a note to say precisely what fault was penalised.

Ian Smith and I were also in the observation hut, on site, where the judges deducted marks for faults and Eric recorded them on his chart and I discuss them with both Ian and Eric before going out to interview the competitors after their runs.

Although I lay no claims to being an 'expert' in the art of trialling, I can therefore shape my interviews to match the truly expert reactions of the judges, hopefully extracting constructive comments from the shepherds about the specific difficulties they experienced and these interviews will, of course, be included with the tape of the whole run, Ian being present when we discuss it and able to ask me to get them to expand on any features which he can see will make good television.

When the whole material is returned to London, there is considerably more than can be fitted into the finished programme because we have no way of controlling the length of each run, which is normally a few minutes longer than can be accommodated but has, in exceptional cases, been more than half an hour!

As with writing, most programmes benefit from 'sharpening-up' by removing the less dramatic or important parts so Ian spends literally days on end, in cutting the tape down to length.

Eric's plan of each run, with the crucial, mark-losing faults marked against the spots where they happened, serves to dictate the vital shape for the run but, when the superfluous portions are removed, the action is left as a staccato series of sections of the run which would be totally unacceptable as a finished record.

To illustrate this, a dog might take half a minute to drive his sheep in a straight line between two gates, which would be boring to watch. So the piece where he starts is left, the dull middle section is cut, to the entrance to the next gate or other obstacle, saving perhaps twenty-five seconds. Simply by inserting a cut-away shot of a close-up of the dog or the shepherd blowing his whistle or other apparent irrelevance, the gap in the middle is lost and the action shows the dog driving sheep, in long shot, with a glimpse of his or his master's expression in close-up, merging into smooth action at the next obstacle so that viewers are unaware that twenty-five seconds of less interesting drive with no important incident has gone onto the cutting room floor.

However simple such an exercise may sound in theory, the fact is that there are cats' cradles of tape to be sorted and shaped to give a fair picture of the judges' markings, even when the runs have been shortened. The atmosphere is created by blending in shots of scenery, spectators, close-ups of dogs and handlers and the whole mosaic of the home backgrounds of competitors, their families, their stock and way of life. To break up long sequences of several trials, the action is laced with the 'rural magazine' inserts recorded before the trials were run. It is comparable to constructing and assembling a giant, sophisticated jigsaw puzzle.

When all this has been done, Ian is joined in a highly specialised suite of electronic equipment by a skilled VT editor who edits the master tapes to follow the plot he has shaped.

This final record, as seen by viewers, is not of course available until editing is complete so that it is not possible for Eric to add his final commentary until that stage. If he gave a 'live' commentary, on the spot, as the trial evolved, his words which covered parts of the run which were subsequently axed would be chopped out of the dialogue, making it a nonsense.

So we record the whole eight programmes, on site, in September, and go to London four times after the original has been edited. There we run the finished programme through a few times, I dub on commentary to any magazine items which are not already covered by sound, and Eric does his commentaries, not as they happen at the time but as the camera has recorded them and the editor prepared them for transmission.

This time our roles are reversed. In September I 'top and tail' each of the eight programmes 'live' to camera, chat to winners and losers after each run, do an odd magazine item or so, and introduce whoever presents the prizes. Eight programmes, in five and a half days, is high production, by anybody's standards. For a rural old josser like me, who makes no pretence at being a slick TV professional, it pushes things to the limit. I am not, by nature, a worry-guts and don't get consciously steamed-up. But the adrenalin flows so freely that, by about Thursday night, I can't unwind and don't get much more sleep until I get home on Saturday.

Eric has it easier, on site, because he is mainly occupied in making notes on each run, so that, when the time comes to dub his commentary on the edited tape, his notes are copious enough to remind him of what happened, back in September, and he can do a spontaneous running commentary to silent tape instead of when it happens. All that we do together on site, is to chat about the course and make a few predictions on form. Apart from acting as a 'trailer', this also introduces him to viewers, who can then put a face to the voice of his out-of-vision commentaries, instead of having to listen to anonymous, disembodied patter.

What we lose by being just ordinary countrymen, with no pretensions that we are chromium-plated professionals, we more than make up in our relations with competitors and their friends.

Eric is known to them all because sheep and sheep dogs are his life, and by being at trials almost every weekend, he is not just 'accepted' as being a member of the sheep dog world, he is among the leading lights. Being introduced, by Eric, as a pal of his – and having a lifetime's experience of working (but not sheep) dogs of my own, I too am accepted on an equal footing, sharing common interests.

From the programme's point of view, this is of critical importance. So many smart-arses among professional interviewers believe that success at their craft produces 'hard' interviews, which bare the souls of their subjects, leaving them looking like knaves or fools. If nobody is 'sent up', it is, by their standards a 'soft' and unsuccessful interview.

Eric and I appreciate our luck in working in marvellous countryside, with a bunch of thoroughly delightful people. I do not 'interview' them, in the hard news sense, but simply chat with them instead, allowing viewers to overhear our conversation. I have so much in common with the chaps I meet that they feel that they know me well enough to trust me. They pay me the compliment of talking without the inhibiting necessity of weighing words which the slickies might use to trip them up. I enjoy the exercise as much as they do, and we meet again and again, in subsequent years, in the certainty that each will welcome the other, when we cross paths again.

The stage managers are simply vital links in this chain. We have two of them, one who is mainly absorbed in checking that everything out on the course is functional and in good order. He has a 'walkie-talkie' with which he can pass and receive information with the producer, director and shepherds in the release pen, who turn out the right-sized packet of sheep from the main reservoir for every run, and gentle them towards the lift post. When the director tells him that all cameras are ready for a run, he sees the competitor and his dog are waiting within a few yards of the start post and gives the word to release the sheep. When they are moving in the right direction, he beckons the competing shepherd and his dog to come up to the start post, from which they will both be able to see the sheep the dog will have to fetch. The shepherd is then told he can start his dog when he is ready, and cameras roll, to the director's instructions, and a record is made of the run as it happens.

Keith Hatton, the other stage manager, is in charge of Eric and me. He comes from Wales, and takes on the job year after year, jollying and encouraging me until I am almost deluded into thinking I'm doing fine.

'Topping and tailing' often don't work to plan, as in the first programme, at Buttermere, when soapboxes had to be fetched for me to stand on to save the horizon decapitating me! With so many programmes in a series, it is often difficult to avoid appearing in the same place twice, so producers and directors sometimes scrape the barrel to dig up something new.

I have been asked to stand on slippery rocks, in the river's shallows, 'because the reflections are so good'; or to lean on a gate, standing in proud isolation with no fence either side, so that the wise go round it and only fools go through. Once I was perched on a rock, with the ground dropping sheer away to the valley below, and, as my head for heights is limited to standing on a chair seat to put in a new electric bulb, there was more chance that I would throw up than pour out welcoming honeyed words to seduce our, viewers.

Keith Hatton is a tower of strength on such occasions. He can charm the birds out of the trees and, whatever catastrophe looms, he is always capable of fooling me that everything is going fine. Or he always was capable of such subterfuge, though now I know him so well, there are a few small clues when all is not precisely as it seems!

He has a genuinely friendly, open smile, but, just occasionally, one side of his face looks happier than the other, or his eyes glaze over. Either is a danger signal.

I have a positive flair either for getting names wrong or forgetting them altogether at the last critical moment, so that I sometimes make the most dreadful cock-ups, as when I introduced an interviewee as Heartburn instead of Fairbairn. It had arisen because some wag had dreamed up the nickname when we arrived and it had been an in-joke all week.

So I sailed gaily into my spiel without noticing my lapse – though the interviewee did. After a bit, Keith drew his finger across his throat, which is a normal way of instructing me that an interview will be

*Keith Hatton mikes me up for interview. Eric is joining us.*

aborted for any reason from a technical hitch to overrunning, though rarely because the chap on his feet has forgotten the name of his victim!

Eric, who has a wry sense of humour, takes my misfortune – or mismanagement – as hilarious, and often adds fuel to the fire with some quip of his own. Nobody else sees the joke because any duplication caused by incompetence adds to unavoidable pressures with such a tight schedule.

50

Poor Keith is the nut between the nutcrackers. He knows that my gaffe was accidental, however inexcusable, and he is always anxious not to aggravate the odds on a repetition by saying anything to shatter my concentration. Pouring into his earphones is a torrent of vitriol from the director or Ian. Directors and producers don't like being held up by presenters who ham interviews or introductions.

The result is a pantomime act such as is so often shown on the television news when a reporter is holding forth with some ignorant foreigner who can't speak plain English.

The reporter asks a question and then there is a wooden puppet show while an interpreter transposes it to words his master can comprehend. The foreigner then gabbles at the interpreter, while the reporter puts on an unconvicing act of intelligent anticipation. Then the interpreter relays what the dignitary is supposed to have said, though I often suspect he is simply spouting the party line and what he says may bear little relationship to what the boss man really said or meant to say.

Keith Hatton is like that. After some hiccup, I see him listening to the tirade from the scanner, and the more lethal it is, the more glazed his expression. When at last it dries up, the glaze broadens into a grin, and he simply says 'Sorry about that. We've got to do it again. Just a technical hitch, a hair on the camera lens or something. No fault of yours, of course. They do hope you don't mind!' After years on the job, I know better. 'Come off it,' I say. 'Let's hear what they really said!' We now know each other well enough for him to spiel out the whole truth, warts and all, and we have a good laugh – and do it right next time.

Ian Smith wouldn't have got so far if he wasn't an exceptional team leader. The crew is large enough to be recruited from several regions, so that there is ample scope for rivalry or feelings that 'the others' – whoever they may be – are receiving favoured treatment.

The engineering manager – a vital job – may come from one region, some of the riggers, who lay out hundreds of yards of cable, may be based elsewhere. Theirs is one of the most thankless tasks in the unit, because the worse the weather, the harder they will have to work. Rain has an almost unconquerable tendency to seep in where cables join, putting an irreplaceable camera out of action at the most critical point in a trial. Shots explaining the most vital phase of a contest are irretrievable when the moment has faded. So, however wide the heavens have opened, however chilly the morning, the poor riggers

have to locate the faults and cure them, whatever the discomfort. When it happens, of course, it is always someone else's fault and it needs the wisdom of Solomon to smooth it over.

One camera crew usually comes from Bristol so that they are accustomed to natural history filming, and spot interesting, unrelated subjects during the inevitable intervals between filming the vital action of the trial. These can often be edited in as cutaways, to help link items in the final programme, and we have had marvellous cameos of nuthatches splitting hazel nuts, buzzards soaring high overhead, a pack of fell hounds hunting fox in the crags high over the running ground. Other cameras 'capture' portraits among the small band of knowledgeable spectators. One memorable shot immortalised a low-slung lady with her low-slung Basset Hound, confirming the belief that dogs look like their owners. Other shots etch graphic portraits of suspense, as wives and girlfriends share their menfolk's traumas, when some unexpected rebel ewe cocks-up a winning trial.

In one programme, I set the scene and introduced competitors in an almost tropical downpour, but the quality of modern cameras is so superb that every feature of my face was as sharp as if the sun was shining. I was watching the programme closely, on the box – for I have no fiercer critic – when I noticed what looked like a metal stud in the lobe of my ear. Nothing is calculated to make me blow a gasket more surely than pansy modern youths, who have Mohican hairstyles, necklaces and earrings. I yearn to pick them up and shake them, to see if they rattle, to diagnose their sex. The vision of my phizog, filling the screen, with the lobe of one ear apparently pierced and bejewelled, appalled me. As I watched, the 'jewel' literally grew before my eyes, elongating into a perfect 'pear drop', until it swelled beyond the powers of surface tension to sustain it, and fell, with a 'plop', to the ground.

The cameraman had had a ball and, when he noticed the raindrops running down my cheeks, he had concentrated on one huge drop accumulating on the lower surface of my ear, till the force of gravity had eventually triumphed over his aesthetic eye and his camera's artistry captured its disintegration.

When we started the series, back in 1975, we were so much out of our depth that it stretched us past the limit. Being required to think

---

*Steve Morris, the director, leaves his scanner and comes down onto the course to discuss tactics with me.*

*Andy Bloomfield comes to make a pictorial plan of the course, showing all obstacles. This plan is used at morning briefings to show competitors, and Eric uses it in the programme to give viewers a plan of the course. Arrows are shown at intervals during trials to pinpoint position of sheep and dogs.*

on my feet, improvising dialogue to suit constantly changing circumstances, took all my concentration. The same interviews or comments would have sounded far better if they had been simpler and less highly polished.

Working for a producer who is prepared to stomach a few gaffes in the interests of a more spontaneous atmosphere has slackened the tensions until the job genuinely becomes a relaxed pleasure.

We always find ourselves booked into a friendly and comfortable hotel where it is bliss to wallow in a hot bath before reassembling in the bar for a civilised drink – and work again.

Ian's habit is to get everyone together before dinner to go through next day's stint – which actually consists of one programme on Tuesday and Saturday, and two – one morning and one after lunch – on Wednesday, Thursday and Friday.

Minor hiccups today must be avoided tomorrow. My links, to camera, connecting magazine items filmed elsewhere, have to be tailored to fit, and the general topics mentioned in introductions and pay-offs agreed. I never script them, precisely for the simple reason

54

that I make no pretence of being an actor and am far happier talking more or less off the top of my head.

Having worked hard all my life, I know of few jobs so sapping or so stimulating. Living on the edge of a wood which I manage as a reserve for wildlife, time is more often measured by calendars than by clocks. If friends promise to come 'on Sunday, at eight o'clock,' I expect to see them at eight o'clock, but am not sure which Sunday until they arrive.

Television is a medium of short bursts of intense activity separated by endless periods of enforced idleness. I once did a tele-commercial, where I was required to talk for fifteen seconds but had to hang around three and a half hours to do so, until the shadow of a stone wall behind me fell at the precise angle the producer wanted. When the time arrived, a cloud crept over the sun – and we had to wait another twenty-four hours before being galvanised into momentary action!

No such extravagance is tolerated by Ian Smith, but some delays are inevitable, if only because cameras are occupied recording scenic shots or other peripheral material, to be edited into the finished programme.

I always welcome such interludes because they allow me to wander round, getting to know competitors and spectators, our farmer hosts, and the chaps who supply and marshal the sheep. They are the most delightful bunch of countrymen it is possible to imagine, and my casual conversations with them have sparked off friendships beyond price.

*The morning briefing of competitors, attended by Ian and Eric (who brief them about the course).*

# 3
# One Man

IF IT IS THE stunning scenery which first hooks casual viewers, it is the competitors and their dogs who really land the fish.

Loneliness is the backcloth against which such men spend a great deal of their lives. They make their living shepherding sheep in steep, inhospitable country, often so hard and rocky that machinery of any sort would be shattered and broken within hours of intruding into such solitudes.

Herbage to sustain the flock is so sparse that it is necessary to range over hundreds of acres to pack their bellies. Shepherds know that sheep are as profligate as men and that they will seek the best pasture to exploit it beyond the point of regeneration so that poor land will decline to desert.

Proper management of both flock and vegetation needs a clever shepherd, to move his sheep on to pastures new, while there is still enough growth left in the old, not only for it to recover, but to thrive and thicken in his care.

The life is lonely and demanding, so that hill shepherds are real men – in the fullest sense. They need great stamina to spend day after day walking miles across such inhospitable terrain, so that rain or sweaty sunshine must make no difference. Endless hours without human conversation leave more time than enough for thought, though shepherds would certainly scoff at anyone who floated the notion that they are nature's philosophers! Such loners, who often need sharp wits and great physical endurance are, of necessity, extremely self reliant.

I am lucky enough to get to know many of them so well that our respect is mutual and they are confident that I will not bowl them a verbal googly which might show them up before their friends.

It is easy – and very pleasant – as a result, to chat to them perfectly naturally, either before or after they run their dogs in competition. Faced by a more conventional smart-arse 'reporter', they would either clam up entirely, answering silly questions with equally silly monosyllabic answers till the biter was bit and dried up too, to the huge delight of any intelligent audience. Or, if he really riled them, they would give at least as good as they got, though their natural country courtesy would impel them to cocoon their comments so that what they said would be far less offensive than what they did not say.

Thirteen annual series have been enough to make mutually trusted friends, so that we can discuss the performance of man and dog in as relaxed a fashion as if there was not a TV camera in the county.

It is immensely important to them that they acquit themselves with distinction, because our television trials are held in the highest respect, not because winning is of greater intrinsic worth than winning any other major trial, but because, instead of a few hundred spectators, there will be millions watching, among whom will be not only all their friends but many of their rivals.

Such self reliant men talk freely about the butterflies in their tummies before the trial commences. They are probably out 'trialling' almost every weekend of the year and, in Wales or the North of England or Scotland, there may be several trials, on the same day, all within a radius of twenty miles or so.

This is not the cut-throat catastrophe it might seem, because, instead of one trial scooping all the competitors in the district, many men will run a dog in one trial, jump in the car and run another, or sometimes two more, trials at other events – and be back at the first to hear the results of their earlier efforts. The day may be a round of activity, where competitors can win – or lose! – several events by nightfall.

It might be thought that ours would be just another notch on their piles of success or failure, but the exposure it gets makes it supremely important in their eyes. Yet, when we have our post mortem, after the event, there are no histrionics, by the winner, nor excuses from the losers.

Chaps who had butterflies often blame themselves, because there is a genuinely telepathic relationship between one man and his dog. A master's nerves can be communicated to his dog, ruining its performance, though it may be several hundred yards away.

When the competitor is controlling his dog by voice commands, this is perfectly understandable. A chap in a flap is likely to talk in staccato monosyllables and it is easy for human bystanders to pick up the tension in his voice, far easier for his dog's more acute hearing and perception.

If he whistles commands on his fingers, it is still conceivable that his stress will be obvious, because the notes will alter – and no dog is at ease when his master is het-up.

It is less easy to understand through what line of communication indecision is transmitted from the mass-produced metal or plastic whistles which so many use.

So I often ask a competitor who has fared less well than we expected, how taut he was before he started. It must be quite embarrassing for men to confess that they are not as hard-boiled as they seem, and that a trial failed more because of them than through any fault of their dog. Their very frankness stamps them as being real men, big enough to admit it when they let their dogs down instead of the reverse. How different from the whinging digs of politicians, forever blaming the other side, or noggin-headed football managers, making lame excuses for the louts they train.

Shepherds often added a delightful spice of humour to embellish their discomfiture. In one trial, a competitor had a couple of sheep in his bunch which really were bloody-minded. They bolted when the rest were docile, and hung back when the dog tried to hurry the laggards up. In the shedding ring and pen they were insolent extroverts. Man and dog made very heavy weather of it, and everyone was sorry for them.

When I talked to the competitor afterwards, I naturally tried to ease him into it, stating the obvious, that he really had had an exceptional bunch of rebels. A sly grin slid over his face and, apropos of nothing, he said in his lovely Scottish brogue, 'I had a lovely Herdwick chop for my supper last night. I'm looking forward to Swaledale chops tonight!'

The relationship between man and dog is bound to be close because both spend so much time, in wild places, totally alone except for each other's company.

Experience, with my own dogs, has been that such close companionship breeds a telepathic harmony where thoughts and mood can be conveyed without any need of words. I own a ninety-acre wood, which I manage as a reseve for wildlife, and the dogs obviously

*Drabble interviews a competitor after his trial.*

enjoy coming with me when I patrol it, as I do every day. It would be unnecessarily dull for them if I made them walk to heel, as characterless as shadows, but, equally obviously, I can't let them amuse themselves by chasing everything that moves. So we compromise. They are allowed to chase – and catch, if they can – rabbits and grey squirrels. They are not allowed to riot after deer or pheasants! Nor are they allowed to shove their snouts up the tunnels of my badger setts, because badgers think less highly of dogs than I do.

When going round the wood, I often wish to check whether a particular sett is or is not occupied, the normal test being whether there are signs of bedding being taken in or fresh earth excavated. Before approaching the sett, I always turn to the dogs and signal them to lie down, in which posture they remain until I call them on again. I began to notice, when turning to give this command, that Tick, a particularly favourite old German Short Haired Pointer, had always beaten me to the punch. By the time I caught her eye, I was always too late, for she was already lying down. Trying to convince myself I knew the answer, I persuaded myself that I usually planned to examine a sett before setting out, and concluded that this must make some tiny difference in my behaviour which the old bitch was sharp enough to fathom. Then I noticed that, even if I had not anticipated examining a sett, and stopped, spontaneously, to do so, the old girl was still a jump ahead and already lying down before I could raise my hand in silent but visual command. I was left with the conclusion that she had stolen the thought off the back of my mind.

She confirmed the possibility in the house. She always slept in a dog-bed in the kitchen, and when I came down in the morning, she was usually, but not always, waiting by the door with a slipper or oven glove, or similar little 'present', to express her delight at meeting me again. She always did so when I was feeling fine, but if I had had a heavy night and woke up disagreeable, there was no canine greeting when I opened the kitchen door. Instead, the old lady would still be stretched in mock slumber, one eye open just enough to test how the land lay before deciding whether to greet me effusively or to bide her time until she had the invitation. Nip, my current favourite bitch, is equally astute in sizing up the situation. She is a sensitive soul who will play me up when I'm in a good mood, but never take the slightest risk of putting a foot wrong when she assesses I'm feeling edgy.

Shepherds' dogs must have even more time and scope to get on beam with their bosses. Sometimes they are required to gather the whole flock and bring it down to the farmstead so that every sheep

*Waiting their call to stardom.*

can be dipped or wormed or sheared. The wisest old ewes may be less than keen and lie-up between rocks or in a gully or otherwise concealed, in the hope that their absence will not be noticed, so that they cower in concealment, hoping not to be discovered.

The shepherd himself can't see them. He may be half a mile or more away, on some friendlier, more accessible slope, so that he can't tell his dog to go on or back, or to right or left. The dog may be as invisible to him as are the sheep, so that he has to rely on the dog's initiative to seek out the stragglers as well as rounding up the more co-operative majority.

Such round-ups will be relatively exceptional. Far more often the object will simply be to move the flock onto fresh pasture, to keep the whole sheep walk in good heart by disciplined rotation. There will now be no hurry, so that man and dog can move the flock on gently, allowing them to graze and crop any surplus as they go. The whole exercise loses any semblance of master and dog, becoming instead a true partnership of one man and his dog, where deep respect and admiration is mutually bestowed.

It produces genuine characters who are the lifeblood of our programme, and the camera, far from dissecting their weakness as so often happens on the box, introduces them to viewers who feel as pleased and privileged as I do to meet them. Their life, on the hills, is hard enough in high summer. In winter it can be horrific.

One chap I know, who lives in an isolated farm on the Pennine Way, gave a graphic description of the tremendous snows in 1947. His wife was in labour, but there was no way that an ambulance could reach them, so the doctor struggled up to the farm on the back of a carthorse. He performed a Caesarian operation by the light of an oil lamp, upon the kitchen table. Neighbours supplied extra saucepans to sterilise the instruments.

Of course, that was forty years ago and Land-Rovers have revolutionised life in remote places which could previously be reached only on horseback in bad weather. Shepherds in the sort of territory which can only be farmed with clever sheepdogs, still live in primitive conditions which would make city social workers scream for legislation.

You can't conquer such weather, so many hill farms have a number of small fields, ranging from one to five acres, situated around the farmstead, where their sheep can at least shelter from it. The land is usually so rocky in hill country that it is possible to pick many tons of random-shaped rocks off the land – and every rock picked up leaves its own area for grass to grow which was a slab of barren rock before.

Because of these rocks, and the shallow skithering of soil which covers them, it has never been possible to cultivate such land. Steel plough shares are no match for such resistance. So there are long periods between lambing and shearing and dipping and worming, when the main task is to 'look' the flock, night and morning, to check that all is well, and to move sheep on to pastures new, to allow the ground just grazed to recover and regenerate.

Diligent farmers, at such times, filled in spare days and weeks by hand-picking stones from the land to expose a little more soil to grow an extra mouthful or so of herbage.

Something has to be done with the stones picked. Put in piles, they will be mere monuments to ineffective labour, because they will blanket growth in large patches as surely as they covered a myriad small patches before they were picked. The sensible alternative is to build them into dry stone walls, enclosing small paddocks near the farmstead, where grazing can be controlled by rotating from one paddock to the other, and where the whole flock can be folded when harsh winters make it impossible to find them on the open hills – or for them to find food beneath the snow.

Logical as this might sound, success depends on bringing the flock down to the homestead before the tempest blows. The weatherman on the wireless is useless enough down in the lowlands, where large areas are so similar that there seems some chance that the weather they will enjoy (or suffer!) will be uniform. Predictions before the major news bulletins infuriate me by pretending to forecast what it will be like next week – or even tomorrow. If my predictions, as a journalist, were as unreliable, I should soon find myself among the spending cuts! The chances of success 'next week' are even more remote, and, in hill country, prophecy is a certain non-starter, because we often notice, when recording *One Man and His Dog*, that it is bucketing with rain 'our' side of the hill and brilliant sunshine across the valley. Or, less often, vice versa!

Never being one to take enough care to avoid dropping embarrassing bricks, I was once caught out on a 'live' Breakfast Time television programme by careless talk of weathermen.

I had been muttering with the presenter about our latest series, due to start that night, when he threw in the question 'You're an old countryman, Phil. What sort of weather do you forecast?'

62

If I'd been on my toes, I should have realised it was simply a device to link our interview to the next item on the programme, which was the Official Weather Forecast – with Important capital letters!

Not being on my toes, I stumbled right into it and replied that my grandmother's corns were more reliable portents than the weatherman on the wireless. By that time the weatherman was standing directly behind me, with his abracadabra and his complicated charts, but I am happy to say he was far more embarrassed than I was! Too near the bone, perhaps?

Hill shepherds can't afford to make many mistakes, and they are out in the wilderness so much that they gradually accumulate a whole collection of small observations, which might mean nothing nationally or long term, but really do give at least a few hours notice of local impending storms. The wind blowing from this hill, or clouds over that, soon ring bells of prophecy; the mistlethrush, or thrice cock, is known as the storm cock where I come from, and his repetitive, melodious song is our warning as well as nature's symphony. Every shepherd has his own pet theories, which may be demonstrably false where you or I live, but mean more than 'official' forecasts to him. Nevertheless, the weather is so capricious that the wisest countryman and the most scientific bearded boffin often come unstuck.

When this happens in winter, shepherds and their dogs set out on the most dangerous and skilled of all the tasks recorded in the calendar. Somewhere under the limitless white blanket of snow upon the hills, sheep will be invisible because they are buried, sometimes many feet under the snow.

All sorts of gimmicks are used to locate them. Steel bars grope and probe, indicating success when the bar, slipping effortlessly into a drift, is not brought up sharp because it hits rock or frozen soil. The spongy, woolly fleece is felt instead, and confirmation of the discovery will be that a tuft of wool will be sticking to the probe when it is withdrawn.

Intimate knowledge of the terrain reminds the shepherd precisely where gullies and hollows are concealed, which sheltered fugitive sheep in previous storms, so he knows just where to probe or dig with the greatest chance of success. Sheep too young to remember the last bad storm are still likely to lie-up in the same refuges as their predecessors, because the instinct which guides one generation to select the safest spots will not fail successors down the years.

Time is not of the essence because sheep marooned in snowdrifts are not in the same peril of frostbite as we would be. The lanolin in their fleece is a marvellous waterproofing agent, and the woolly fleece itself is a sure blanket against cold. Furthermore, the grass under deep snow is easier to eat and digest than it might have been on the surface, where it could have been frozen and unpalatable. But, if sheep are too bunched under snow, they may suffocate each other or pile on top of each other, causing aborted lambs. They would be safer and easier to supervise nearer the homestead, and good shepherds know that no brilliant gimmick to locate them is half as good as a good dog, which will listen for movement and breathing, and the coarse belches when food is regurgitated as undigested cud, to be chewed and enjoyed at leisure. Good dogs will pick up the faint scent of sheep through porous snow, and they will show the shepherd where to dig by scratching down, as wild hunting dogs will disinter their quarry.

A dog which locates and helps to rescue sheep buried in deep drifts of snow, strengthens the deep bond between man and dog, whose lives are already inextricably entwined.

The stone-walled paddocks round the homestead are neither as bleak nor as inhospitable as they might seem. Fifty yards or so to windward, and parallel to exposed roads in hill country, it is common to see lines of chestnut pale fencing, put there to prevent snowdrifts on the road. When windborne snow hits the open fencing, the fragile screen simply slows it down, causing it to be deposited in snowdrifts which peter out before reaching the road and blocking it.

Dry stone walls work in the same way. They are simply – though very skilfully – made by piling flat rocks on top of each other to a height of four or five feet. Looked at against sunrise or sunset, the light filters through the stones, so that chinks the width of the wall become obvious. Bureaucratic building inspectors would class them as inferior workmanship, but knowledgeable countrymen know that, provided vandals do not demolish them deliberately, they are works of art which will stand the test of time. Never was such permanence fashioned so precariously!

If a solid wall was built, with conventional mortar, the wind would simply swirl over the top of the wall and batter down at whatever shelters on the leeward side as furiously almost as if no wall was there. But, when it hits the looser built obstruction, some wind filters through, slowing the attack, as a parachute cast out behind a landing aeroplane is able to bring it to a standstill on a shorter runway.

Such stone walls are therefore vitally important to sheep husbandry in the hills, not only as a means of clearing ground to grow more

64

*Eric and I go aloft with Keith to Ian's observation hut for briefing. There is another platform above the hut for a camera to give a bird's eye view of the course.*

pasture, but also as a shelter when the flock has to be brought down from the hills in winter storms.

I talked to a delightful 'character' who is a past master in the art of making traditional Cotswold stone walls. He had repaired about five yards of wall that had been vandalised by ramblers, producing an edifice that looked as if it would now withstand a charge of tanks. 'You've made a fine job there,' I said. 'How long do you reckon that it will last?' He eyed it critically and gave the matter due thought before replying, straight to camera, 'I hope it's still standing when I'm paid, on Friday night.'

A vital part of every series is visiting competitors at home. It is a fact of life that viewers enjoy getting personally involved and love watching pleasant people who they feel they know. So, if viewers have paid a privileged visit to the homes of competitors, they feel they know them personally, and become as involved as if competitors they are watching had really welcomed them to their homes.

So, before a competitor comes to the trials field, Ian Smith takes a camera crew to his farm and simply makes a short film about his home and interests.

Viewers – or Ian Smith, who is standing in for them! – are welcomed by the competitor's wife, who may be busy baking cakes for the next Women's Institute meeting, or feeding the dogs, or exercising her horse, or collecting the eggs, or any of the endless tasks that country women cope with.

The children will be about, playing with the latest litter of sheep dog puppies, or bottle-rearing a cade lamb, or practising for the school concert, or driving a tractor so gigantic that they seem no bigger than a tomtit on a round of beef.

Meanwhile, Ian records reams of 'wildtrack' comments by the boss. It is a specialist form of film making, at which he excels, because his questions are so phrased that they can be edited out of the finished film, leaving the subject apparently soliloquising about his farm and his problems, his failures and successes, hobbies and sidelines.

Such country folk are often very good at describing the hows and whys of the physical work they do, but find it less easy to discuss abstract philosophy. I know, from experience, that there will be no problem in getting a shepherd to explain precisely why it is necessary to dock – or cut off – lambs' tails in the lowlands, where flies would lay eggs on them and the hatching maggots would feed upon their living flesh, but that there are heights in the hills above the fly-line where full-tailed sheep would not be so tormented.

But ask the same chap an introspective question, about what satisfaction he gets from being an exponent of such an ancient craft, and he would probably be less forthcoming. It may be that he is too shy to risk ridicule by baring his soul to strangers, who might not understand. Or perhaps he finds it difficult to describe what he cannot physically touch or see or hear.

Yet these short cameos of family life are often revealing, without the need for many words to pad them out. A lad of ten or twelve, day-dreaming about being a Trials champion, when we are dead and gone, can convey more by a casual glance at his puppy or by subconsciously stroking its ear, than by any words to describe their mutual affection. When he grows up and achieves the ambition of his lifetime by winning the Supreme International trophy, all he will say to the dog that shares his triumph is a laconic 'That'll Do'.

Such understatements to express their strongest emotions are typical of these modest men and they shine out, time and again, from the short films Ian makes in their homes.

It becomes a privilege to share their simple pleasure and the fact that their wives never actually tell us how many hours a week it takes to keep the impressive display of silver cups and trophies so shining bright, does nothing to devalue the pride of the whole family in winning them.

Small things like mum baking cakes for invaders from the BBC illustrate just how self-sufficient real country life still is, despite intruding commuters and yuppies and do-gooders, who seem to think that countryfolk are a bunch of simpletons who will be 'deprived' until their villages are ponced up with street lights and public loos, bridge clubs and sports complexes.

They are ignorant of the fact that the Women's Institute is one of the most powerful rural pressure groups in the land, perfectly capable of cracking the resistance of the slickest politicians. The ridiculous media image of the Jam-and-Jerusalem mentality is nothing to be ashamed of, as any who could smell the cooking in competitors' homes would readily concede. The Women's Institute is the perfect country club, where members contribute a pittance to participate instead of the fortune the pseudo-prestigious clubs extort for 'membership'.

Competitors who tell tales of sires and grandsires who shepherded sheep on the same farm put the motorway driven through one man's farm into tragic perspective. The thumbnail sketch, etched by the camera into a mere two or three minutes' narrative, is enough for viewers to feel they know competitors personally when they come to the starting post on the television trials field.

Instead of making clinical assessment of a stranger's performance, it suddenly becomes possible to cast impartiality to the wind and root for one who has become a personal friend, whose wife, we tell our neighbour, is a gifted baker of five-star buns, or whose kids have a natural way with animals, or whose dog, which is just about to run, won the coveted Supreme International last year. Sharing such family secrets almost turns a spectator sport into something in which we, ourselves, can share the successes and the failures.

Not, I might say, that we are ever likely to share the necessary skills, because I often think they must have been inherited to give top shepherds such a start over the most gifted in-comers to the sport.

Any real 'dog-man' can train a dog. All that is needed is enough sympathy and instinctive dog sense to get inside a canine mind – and limitless patience and persistence. Having always been involved with dogs myself, and not suffering fools gladly, I reckon I could train a sheep dog – which is well on the way the day it is weaned, through generations of selective breeding. But having the most perfectly trained dog is only the beginning of winning a trial. The skills of a naturalist and stockman are equally important.

Sheep, as any schoolboy knows, are 'flock' animals, and the language is full of folklore about 'following like sheep', 'as stupid as a sheep', and similar nonsense. Sheep do not naturally 'follow' and they are certainly not stupid, as anyone who tried to win a trial would soon discover. They are not even totally domesticated, because they still retain many of the instincts of their feral ancestors.

Hill sheep are not fenced in like sheep in the artificial fields of the lush lowlands, but are free to wander where they will, so they become highly territorial. Theirs, like ours, is a matriarchal society gaffered by dominant females, so that each ewe tries to choose her own territory. She lambs there and her young ewes are retained as future breeding stock, and grow up to regard the terrain where they were born and reared as their territory for the future. They stay around as family groups from one year to the next and, as the breeding performance of old ewes declines, they go to the butcher, leaving their lambs 'hefted' to the area, which therefore needs no fences and is a great asset to the farm. When the shepherd 'folds' them over to fresh pasture, the grazing they leave recovers and they drift back when the discipline of man and dog relaxes.

When a trial such as ours is to be run, the flock is gathered and assembled in a 'release' pen from which any number can be driven out for man and dog to show their paces when the competition commences.

Most animals, from domestic hens to man, have a social hierarchy or 'pecking order'. The obscenities of intensive poultry husbandry are aggravated because hens are instinctive bullies, who trample and peck their weaker sisters unmercifully. However intolerable the crowded conditions of their battery cage may be, the strong make matters even worse for the weak, who have nowhere to go to find peace or seclusion.

Dogs are 'pack' animals, naturally subservient to their pack leader, which will be the strongest and fiercest, most aggressive animal in the pack. When age weakens him, his successor will subdue him, so that his declining weeks or months give him a taste of the misery he has meted out to others. Man is little better, for nations tear each other to pieces in territorial or religious wars, while in intervals of peace the yobs with most muscle in their arms and least brain in their heads slug it out as 'fans' at football matches.

At least the sheep don't fight, except sometimes the rams, flexing their sexual muscles for the most ewes at tupping time. At other seasons, the tups are segregated from the flock – to avoid unseasonal conceptions – and the ewes simply sneak off to what they regard as the best grazing habitat, or where their dams and grand dams grazed, and they live there in contented social groups, with no disturbance except by the shepherd and his dog.

They are occasionally collected and brought to the release pen at the top of the trials field, to act as living pawns in the game of rustic chess. One man and his dog compete with others of their kind to demonstrate their superior skills in driving a fixed number of sheep round and through the obstacles on a formalised course, laid out to provide similar problems to 'real' shepherding.

At our trials, we have about a hundred sheep in the release pen, at the beginning of the day. Many have lived in remote corners of the sheep walk and are strangers to others. They are edgy because of the fear of the unknown, for none knows the fate of those 'released' – or, to be more accurate, driven out – from the release pen. It would be stupid to suggest that sheep have any powers of imagination, so they cannot anticipate fate from a humane killer or the far worse death by ritual slaughter where the elementary humanity of pre-stunning is not practised before their throat is slit.

But the older members of the flock in our release pen will certainly have experienced the indignity of having their fleece sheared, to leave them naked and shivering. Even worse, shearing leaves them strangers to their own unweaned lambs, who do not recognise them without their familiar fleece and take some time to associate the ewe's familiar voice with her unrecognisable body.

Being penned with friends and strangers in the release pen is bad enough. Far worse is the prospect of being tipped out into the unknown when the release shepherds are instructed to drive another packet of sheep to the fetch post on the trials course.

The wisest among the old ewes try to put off the evil hour by crowding to the back of the pen, as far from the gate as possible. The weaker characters among the captives are thus jostled towards the gate and, if the release shepherds turned out the nearest sheep to the gate, with no selection, the weakest, yes-men (or women!) in the flock would all figure in the early runs, while the tough old rebels, the shop stewards of the Ovine Trades Union, would cower in safety until they were all that were left to run the gauntlet for the last competitors.

In theory, therefore, it would be wrong to allow the release shepherds to make any selection among the sheep they liberate. They are always experienced shepherds themselves, perfectly capable of spotting a potential rebel when they see one. They know who the next competitor will be and, human nature being frail as it is, there would always be the temptation, if they were allowed to select at all, to send down a docile bunch when their pals were competing, and a right bunch of stinkers for competitors they did not like!

Everyone in the sheep dog world knows the possibilities so, being practical countrymen, a sensible compromise has been reached.

When the request is received to send down the next bunch, all the sheep in the release pen are stirred round, shifting the cunning ones from their selected safety at the back of the pen, and forcing them to mix with the minor stampede around the pen. When they are mixed as randomly as a pack of shuffled cards, and not before, the gate is opened and the requisite number released.

It is pure chance whether they are docile or flighty, whether they recognise each other or are strangers. They are inched and gentled, to arrive near the fetch post, and when they are steady there, the competitor is given the signal that he can send his dog as soon as he is ready. He and the dog are on their own and the eyes of the judges and spectators watch every move and listen to every whistle thereafter.

This is where the skills of stockmanship come in. The shepherd can send his dog either to the right or left-hand side of the course on his outrun, to get behind the sheep, prior to lifting and fetching them. He will already have made the decision, based partly on which side the dog prefers, partly on the lie of the land which will best keep the sheep in view. He will obviously be guided, too, by what snags and bonuses have been thrown up by previous competitors.

All that will be theory which he will have worked out before the trial begins. The second by second conduct of the trial cannot be decided till his act in the drama unfolds.

70

*A competitor sends his dog away on right hand out run to gather sheep at beginning of trial.*

In our class of event it is safe to assume that all the dogs are so well trained and responsive that they will follow the commands and instructions of his whistle and his voice as reflex actions. They really are so good that the shepherd can forget them, in the supreme confidence that he can rely on their compliance implicitly.

The sheep are his problem – and they are neither trained nor predictable. They may be an easy – or relatively easy! – bunch; they may be a gang of rebels or, probably worst of all, there may be the odd shop steward type among them, which has no interest in sticking with a bunch of strangers and will take the first opportunity to make a break for it, leave the bunch and try to get back to the comrades who managed to stay in the release pen.

If this happens it will be disastrous, so the competitor needs a dog so good he can forget him in the full confidence that any command will be followed by instant action. With that at the back of his mind,

71

he can concentrate all his attention on the sheep by the fetch post, which may be anything up to half a mile away.

This is where a true stockman's eye is indispensable. Concentrating on his distant sheep, he must be able to spot a potential troublemaker from tiny clues which would have eluded Sherlock Holmes. Erratic or staccato action; hanging back or pressing forward; anything that is 'different' must be spotted, for failure here may lose the trial. Once he locates a suspect, commands must be given to the dog to get him on the correct side, in the exact position to prevent any attempt at mutiny or to nip it in the bud.

Sometimes this is easy, at others impossible, perhaps because there is not one odd-ball in the bunch but several, so that, while preventing one insurrection, another erupts on the other side of the bunch.

If this happens, the best of shepherds sometimes get a bit flustered – and this is where the telepathic relationship between man and dog is a liability instead of an asset for, once the man loses concentration, it is a pound to a gooseberry that the dog will, too.

One sheep breaking away from her fellows will incite the rest to mutiny, and it takes the expertise of the most experienced stockman to decide whether to let the rest of the bunch settle and begin to graze while the dog rounds up the rebel, or if the rebel is so bloody-minded that, as with Mahomet going to the mountains, the practical compromise is to take the whole bunch to the rebel and then to re-start from there.

The more trials one watches, the more one appreciates the skills involved. How fast should the sheep be taken round the course? Over enthusiasm, which panics then into a canter, makes it impossible to guide them through the gates, if their leader has decided to go round. Take them too slowly so that they stop to graze if succculent herbage catches their eye, and it will be an untidy stop-go run, probably deviating from the idealised direct line, each time they are disturbed from their meal.

The really top men keep them moving at a steady pace, between comfortable walk and slow trot, which lets them stay on line without moving so fast that it becomes difficult to stop them – for sheep are notorious for having defective brakes!

It is the ability to achieve such fine control which separates the men from the boys, and championships make it look so deceptively easy that casual observers might not appreciate the quality of stockmanship, without Eric's commentary to highlight it.

*Outrun, dog goes wide to get behind his sheep to 'lift' them and 'fetch' them to the shepherd.*

*Coming through fetch gates.*

It is the sort of skill which one might think would take a lifetime of practical shepherding to acquire, but it soon became obvious how much natural flair must be involved as well.

In his visits to competitors in their homes, Ian met the whole family, probed their individual tastes, and produced a cameo which introduced as many facts about them as is possible in the few minutes available. Little girls with lambs or puppies and older girls on ponies, are not only attractive but tell viewers far more about real life in the country than would be possible in words.

Whatever the Health and Safety men digs out of his small print on such matters, boys love playing with machinery – and they are not nearly as stupid as bureaucracy pretends! So sons of the family have learned to drive a tractor by the time their urban counterparts are exhibiting expertise on skateboards or doing 'wheelies' round the block, with the front wheels of their bicycles cocking snooks at coppers.

Some lads – and I was among them – prefer animals to insensate machines. I loved fetching the cows up on a neighbour's farm, and was prepared to pay for the privilege by mucking them out or slicing swedes in the hand-turned rotary cutters which were commonplace in my vintage. But, although I always had a dog, it wasn't a sheep dog.

Our competitors' sons are reared with sheep dogs. They feed puppies almost before they can walk, and amuse themselves working dad's dog to round up mum's hens by the time they are old enough to go to school. Fetching up the hens after tea, to shut them safe from Charlie Fox, is the best job in school holidays.

Instead of longing to be a train driver or sailor when they grow up, sheep farmers' sons relegate pop singers and footballers to suitable low strata and set their sights on winning the Supreme International Championship, with a dog they've bred and trained themselves.

Dad is naturally proud and does all he can to further such ambitions, and we have already met families such as the Longtons, from the Lancaster area, which have fathers, brothers and sons all up to international championship standard.

While introducing the families of competitors to viewers of the programme, Ian met so many youngsters who had had trained sheep dogs as presents, or who had often trained dogs of their own – with more or less help from dad! – that he decided to devote a programme of the series to a Young Handlers Championship. The idea was to choose a youngster, boy or girl, under twenty, from each of the four countries.

74

There is never any problem about choosing them, because they will already be well known in the sheep dog world, probably having competed in, and sometimes won, minor trials against their elders since the age of twelve or so. The cream of them are likely to be picked to represent their country in international competition when only in their teens.

We were a bit patronising at first, and let them run on a slightly easier course, because the last thing we wanted was to discourage them by showing them doing badly when their friends saw them on the screen. We need not have worried, because they have all been good, and some superb, so that we get shoals of letters from viewers, who are delighted to see that there will be no shortage of skill to maintain the ancient art, because it is so obviously in safe hands of the young stars of the future.

There was just one hiccup which should never have happened. A very pleasant girl who competed was approached by officials of the Wool Marketing Board, who wanted her to take part in a publicity stunt which aimed to increase the sales of wool to the Japanese, who were said, already, to be among our largest foreign customers, sales having quadrupled over the last few years.

The idea was to fly the attractive shepherdess to Japan, with a sheep dog and bitch, so that she could give demonstrations to Japanese ladies, in department stores, to illustrate the art of herding sheep.

As a sales gimmick it was different, if not better, but it attracted a great deal of publicity, much of it adverse. The young lady chosen by the Wool Marketing Board to demonstrate her skills had recently appeared in One Man and His Dog Young Handlers Championship, so it was not long before the Japan Animal Welfare Society made their views known to me – loud and clear.

I was told, in no uncertain terms, that the reputation of the Japs for cruelty to dogs was legendary, and I was also told that the Wool Marketing Board had arranged to leave the dogs in Japan when the tour of demonstrations was complete, allegedly because the cost of flying them back and putting them in quarantine was not warranted in the eyes of bureaucracy.

My sympathies were entirely with the dogs and with the Japanese Animal Welfare Society, whose efforts were dedicated to improving the lot of ill-treated animals there. To quibble about the cost of quarantine for a couple of dogs, when it was thought commercially sound to mount a special sales promotion to increase wool sales already topping thirty million pounds seemed like skinning a turd for a farthing.

To make my point more clearly, I decided to write an article about the issue, so, wishing to present the case clearly, I phoned the Board Press Officer to confirm the facts. Within seconds I was transferred to the Managing Director, who was certainly very sensitive about the whole question, so I recorded our conversation in case there was any subsequent confusion between what had been said and what was said to have been said!

He eventually gave me his assurance that the dogs would be regularly inspected by a vet, to ensure they suffered no cruelty, but it did nothing for my gut feeling that no money on earth would persuade me to leave a dog of mine to the tender mercies of natives in the Land of the Rising Sun – and I gather that organisations working for animal welfare in those parts would not disagree with me.

On a purely pragmatic level, the sales promotion of the Wool Marketing Board may be quite adroit, but if the Japs really are among our best customers for wool, it seems daft to me to teach them the ancient arts of shepherding sheep! Even bureaucrats must have heard that, when we taught Japs how to make motor bikes and wireless sets, they soon beat us at our own game, as struggling members of our motor cycle and electronics industries would confirm.

More sophisticated shepherdesses rarely match up to the Dresden china image, but Viv Billingham is a delightful exception. She has a smile which would charm the birds off the trees, a pink-and-white complexion, and a billowing mane of blonde hair. But there the resemblance ends, because shepherding in hostile hill country makes physical demands that none but the toughest can meet, and Viv is outstanding at her job.

She was taken to her first sheep dog trial by her mother when she was four, and her proud achievement, about three years of constant effort later, was learning to whistle on her fingers. (Without mum finding out, because she thought it an unladylike accomplishment!)

For her first employment she took a live-in job on a lonely moorland farm with a canny Yorkshireman who asked her to go on a month's trial – for which he 'paid' her with a pair of foot-blistering new boots!

Her next job was with a skinflint Welsh farmer, who 'didn't like greedy girls', so the fare was pretty sparse. The bed was always damp, there was a bat in the bathroom, which fluttered round the candle, and, to cap all, the farmer took to his bed with brucellosis, leaving an inexperienced Viv solely responsible. She was up at five, often having

76

to milk by hand because the milking machine was so temperamental. She then had to wash the utensils, take the milk to the road with the tractor, feed the calves, truss the hay, shepherd the sheep, muck out the byre, fill the coke hods for the house, and carry water in three-gallon pails for several weeks when the farm water supply packed up.

The one bright spot was that the farm dogs fell for her instinctive kindness and filled her eyes with pleasure as they worked for her.

When the boss eventually recovered, they wouldn't work for him, so he made Viv drive them off. They naturally did not understand her sudden (apparent!) hostility, and the hurt look in their eyes so distressed her that she handed in her notice.

The next twelve years were bliss. Her gaffer was kind and encouraged her, allowing her to keep and work dogs of her own. She has a wry sense of humour, describing a chance romance of her bitch Kim, who ran off and mated with her own father Rob, on the next farm. Rob seems quite a character, for 'he spent his spare moments biting quarrymen, first having knocked them off their bicycles.' she said.

So much for visions of delicate Dresden shepherdesses. The inevitable relaxation for such a lass was going sheep dog trialling, which was where she met Geoff Billingham, her future husband. She fell in love at first sight – with his dog, and at second sight with Geoff, who was a top class triallist himself! They went to live in wild Cheviot country, on the Scottish border, and in 1978 she competed in the Scottish National Trials and she appeared on Ian's little 'family cameo' in 1981 when her husband Geoff ran in both the brace and singles trials of *One Man and His Dog*. When we ran the trials at Bala Geoff won the trophy. In 1982 Viv was picked for the Scottish team in *One Man and His Dog*, coming second in competition against some of the best shepherds in the land.

Her fame was such that, in 1985, she was invited to fly to The States to judge an American sheep dog trial, being asked to give 'a short talk' about what she would be looking for before the trial started. She has written a couple of books about her life (*One Woman and Her Dog*, and *The Shepherd's Wife*), and she described (typically!) her American trip as her American Experience. My guess is that it was at least as memoriable an experience for the Yankees as it was for Viv.

Folk often tell me that I am lucky to meet such 'characters' – because 'characters' are a rare and endangered species in modern times.

'Characters' have never been common – or they would not have stood out as exceptional – but I don't believe they are any rarer now than they were in the past, certainly in deep country. Something-for-nothing scroungers who believe the world owes them a living, gang up together in city streets and football terraces. They would go whinging to the nearest social worker if they were asked to go out in depth of winter to rescue sheep buried in snowdrifts or to gather a flock from wild hills in the height of summer.

The reason that viewers are so pleased to meet the competitors at sheep dog trials is because it shines through that their work really is their pleasure. They enjoy it so much that, when they have finished shepherding on the farm, they go off with their dogs from choice, to match them against other wise dogs and other skilled shepherds, for the sheer luxury of testing their dogs against the best that their friends – and bitter rivals! – can bring.

My friends tell me that I really seem to enjoy myself when we are doing the programme, and it is perfectly true that, apart from the nagging fear that I won't do the programme justice, I really do enjoy it. He would be an ungrateful lout who did not appreciate the privilege of working with such delightful people in such stunning scenery.

Letters that we get, and researched 'appreciation' figures, gleaned from viewers, indicate that I am in no minority, because all nice people do like nice dogs, and real dog-men have a common bond with other dog lovers, whether professional shepherds or humble pet-owners.

Considering how genuinely involved with their dogs such shepherds get, I find the relationship is sometimes very puzzling.

At one end of the scale, Viv Billingham gave in her notice because she was required to discourage a dog which had developed deep loyalty and affection for her, because it was no longer prepared to work for its less sympathetic master. The hurt in its eyes, eloquent of disillusion because she had apparently lost her affection for it, meant more to her than her job, in times when jobs were hard to find.

At the other end of the scale there are a minority of owners who regard dogs as tools of their trade, as expendable as worn-out tractors. All is sweetness and light so long as the dog is on top form, but when age and the toughness of the job slows down the flesh, it will be disposed of, however willing the spirit continues to be.

When a sheep dog, used to years of gentling sheep, begins to show his age, he may well be sold to strangers to finish his useful days on the far tougher job of herding cattle. I belong to the Viv Billingham school of thought. I always keep bitches but have only bred one litter of pups in a pretty long lifetime.

I once had a favourite Stafford bull terrier, Rebel, who was known far and wide for her prowess at ratting, and I was so fond of her that I decided to let her have a belly of pups, without thinking the implications properly through.

Several times she caught over a hundred rats in a day – almost a barrowful – and in more than one season she caught a thousand rats. I basked in the reflected glory of such achievement, and went ratting every Sunday, which I reckoned did me, and the community, far more good than the parson's sermon.

In due course, Rebel produced a fine litter of six pups, which she proceeded to rear in a corner of the kitchen. They were sired by an extremely good dog belonging to a friend, so one was bespoke as the price of the service.

At about six weeks old we considered advertising the remaining five, when it suddenly occurred to us that the instant we had pouched the fiver, which was a high price for a dog in those days, its fate would be completely beyond our control.

My imaginative mind conjured up visions of wandering down some seedy back street and spotting our pup, pining its heart out, chained to a draughty comfortless kennel. Beaten if it barked in protest and neglected if it suffered in silence.

No money could compensate for such nightmares, so some solution had to be found where my wife and I could continue to control their destiny and sleep in peace.

We eventually decided to give them away to owners who seemed to be kind and reliable. Since we had no such guarantee, we protected the pups by trying to cocoon them by three unbreakable conditions attaching to the gift.

If, for any reason, the owner could not or did not want to keep his pup, he must either return it or destroy it, and furnish evidence that he had done so. We felt that putting a cossetted dog down humanely is far kinder than degrading its standard of life by unacceptable conditions.

From the new owner's point of view it was a jolly good way of getting a top class dog but, even so, we found the greatest difficulty in finding five owners who we were confident would treat our pups as well as we would. I never bred another litter!

Perfectly nice and responsible shepherds, who use their dogs day-in, day-out, as essential tools of their trade, might reasonably think that I was going over the top. Their treatment of their dogs is impeccable, they live in precisely the type of outside kennel they would get if passed on to another owner, so that, never having experienced the soft comforts of house dogs, they would tell you that they will not miss what they never had. And, thus, far, they would be right!

Being pack animals, they are psychologically dependent on having a pack leader, to whom they give natural obedience as the pack leader of a pack of wolves would exact. And when, for any reason, that leader fails or disappears, subservient members of the pack would simply transfer their loyalty to his successor.

Trainers of Guide Dogs for the Blind have brought this to a fine art. Puppies are removed from their dam as soon as they are weaned and transferred to separate human 'puppy walkers', who take them home and 'socialise' them by getting them house-trained, tolerant of other dogs, cats, bicycles and other hazards that beset 'family' dogs, so that, by the time they are nine months old and ready for specialist training, they come when called, sit or lie down on command, walk on a lead and are not overawed by traffic, visitors or shopping crowds.

During this period of 'puppy-walking' the pup naturally develops affection for its hostess, who it accepts as a natural pack leader.

So far so good, but if such admiration and affection goes too far there is a danger that it will develop into a one-man-dog and would pine when passed to a trainer or blind owner. To avoid this, it is carefully supervised and passed on to another puppy walker if in danger of becoming too attached to the first.

When passed on to a training centre for highly specialised and professional training, it will find its trainer totally dominant, and may develop unswerving allegiance to him, so that there would be major difficulty when passed, finally as a 'finished' guide dog, to the blind person who would keep it for life.

Well aware of this danger, one trainer will pass on to a colleague any dog which shows signs of growing too devoted, so that, by the time it is passed to its blind owner, it may well have had what it must regard as four or five 'owners' before. It will thus have become fixated to people, in general, rather than to some specific 'one man', so that guide dogs are deliberately trained to be faithful to anyone who holds their harness rather than to a single owner.

There is no such deliberate policy by shepherds with their dogs, but the fact that many shepherds keep quite a large number of dogs in various stages of training means that the dogs have canine as well as human companionship and are able to spread their affections.

80

Herding – or driving – sheep is closely allied to the hunting instinct, and anyone who watches a collie quivering with excitement before being allowed to dash onto the trials field will appreciate that there is simply nothing he would rather do than gaffer a bunch of sheep. It is as attractive, in his eyes, as ratting to a terrier, or shooting to a spaniel, and once a terrier has been blooded on rats he will sell his soul to anyone who has a ferret and a stick.

So it may well be no great hardship for a collie, which is no more than an individual member of a group of other collies, to be passed to another owner, who will keep him under similar conditions and take him shepherding sheep! The real traumas begin when owners and dogs, which for any reason have been inseparable, are parted.

Countrymen and stockmen are sometimes pretty down to earth. The daughters of great friends of ours hand-reared a 'cade' lamb apiece on the bottle, and being practical, if not sentimental lasses, they christened their pets Deep and Freeze!

It says it all about stockmen. We are pretty self-supporting and have never bought an egg in almost fifty years of married life. I buy a dozen day-old chicks every spring, rear them under an infra-red lamp, and run them, free range, in the wood and paddock for sixteen months, until next season's pullets start to lay. We rear cockerels for the table, and run a pig, free range, in the wood. The quality of such naturally produced meat is as superior to the cotton woolly intensively farmed mush from the supermarket as free range eggs are to battery eggs.

I feed the stock myself and know it individually, but so long as I believe it has had a natural and dignified life, I have no compunction when the time comes to put it on the table.

Shepherds, I guess, are the same. They take a deep professional pride in producing prime stock of the quality that gave us the reputation of being the best stockmen in the world. But they regard it as a crop, to be harvested, when it is ripe, and they regard their dogs as essential – and respected – tools of their trade. Such craftsmen take a great pride in their work and it is the ambition of all not only to do the job better than their rivals, but to be seen to do it better. This is what motivates them, after a long and gruelling week's work, to go out on Saturday and Sunday, to do exactly the same thing for pleasure.

With so many competitors, with a lifetime's experience both as stockmen and dog handlers, it is the tiny imperfections or supremacy which can make all the difference between consistent success or near misses. The best man may own only one dog of potential world class

*Andrew Preston, a judge, discusses the merits of the sheep with Eric.*

in a lifetime, and when the dog comes along, it will bequeath fame on its owner for his lifetime. As my terrier conferred on me the proud title of 'the kid wot belongs to the lemon-eyed bitch,' champion shepherds bask in the reflected glory of the dogs who share their fame. When, as sometimes happens, they send such a partner to The States in exchange for a pot of gold, it only goes to show how different our standards are.

One of my few regrets about the side-effects of our television series is that it has inflated the price of winning dogs, contributing to such sales, and encouraged members of the public to buy collies which may be totally unsuitable to the type of life they can offer them.

To win the Supreme International Sheep Dog Trial is the ambition of every competitive shepherd. Every other competitive shepherd will know about it and it is the ultimate accolade among members of the sheep dog world. But the sheep dog world has a restricted orbit. Winning the *One Man and His Dog* television trial is far less important, if only because competitors are invited to compete, as opposed to having competed specifically for the privilege.

The fact remains that far more people see the television trials, and complete strangers send their congratulations to the winner – and possibly apply for a pup.

The fashionable nostalgia for country ways and customs, and the drift from cities to villages, because the in-thing now is to flog a pretentious town house in favour of a cottage in the country, has caused a market explosion in rural assets. Every commuter's kid is now kitted out with a pony, and dad has a gun in the local syndicate shoot and a labrador in the back of his Volvo or Range Rover.

So, when such viewers see the programme, some of them romanticise about a few sheep in the orchard and a sheep dog to prove, to the world and themselves, that they have really arrived in the country.

Even worse, those who are still marooned in city streets, daydream of a cottage in the country – with a collie as tangible proof that they mean business.

Conditions for collies may be less than ideal, as yard dogs on farms of the unimaginative – but it may be even worse for collies confined in flats or villas, while their owners are working in the office.

So, once in every series, I try to put off those who see Eric's 'wisest-dogs-in-the-world' on the television screen and fantasise themselves, with dog and crook, showing the experts how to go on. They then buy a collie pup as the first step. Some we succeed in putting off. Some ignore the plea and regret it, though the poor dog probably regrets it more. A tiny minority make a success of a collie in a town – or think they do – so write rude letters telling me to mind my own business. You can't win 'em all!

Very occasionally indeed we introduce viewers to a top class competitor, who does not make his living as a farmer or a shepherd. The odd postman or schoolteacher or lecturer at an agricultural college keep sheep to train dogs, instead of dogs to shepherd sheep, as Viv Bollingham found on her American Experience.

Whether young handler or skilled old stager, professional shepherd or hobby triallist, it becomes obvious to viewers that contestants at trials have so much in common that their love of dogs and interest in sheep surpass differences of sex or age or status.

As a complete contrast to the dramatic scenery of Lakeland or wild hill country, we held one series at Chatsworth, the Derbyshire estate of the Duke and Duchess of Devonshire.

I have often wondered, when working on such great estates, how the original owners, who chose such spots to live, decided precisely where to site their stately homes. Did they start off with open scenery and plant it with trees, having a clear mental picture in their mind's eye of what their grandchildren's grandchildren would see in centuries to come? Did they say, as they heeled some sapling in, 'This will be a majestic oak or lime, which will dominate the skyline, when two hundred years have passed since the worms converted my remains to rich compost to feed its roots.' Or were they less visionary and more practical? Did they start with unbroken woodland and nibble clearings until they had literally created the matchless scenery which made the great estates of England so far superior to any in the world? Not only is the scenery more consciously beautiful but, in my experience, the owners live up to the standard of their lands.

Beautiful countryside, merely administered, by bureaucrats, who own nothing themselves, as so much Lakeland scenery is, acquires the sourness of impersonal frictions between the tenants, who earn their living there, have little respect for nabobs, who they rightly regard as outsiders. The hereditary owners of great estates are regarded as respected personal friends.

At Chatsworth, the Duke and Duchess of Devonshire would have been perfectly within their rights to delegate their land agent's assistant's personal dogsbody to deal with the likes of us. That is about where we would have figured in the local pecking order.

Not a bit of it. The duke and duchess both mucked-in to add their weight to making the programme a success. The duke not only told me about some of the problems and joys of heading such an enterprise, but was not above poking a bit of fun at himself by recounting how, when he'd been walking in an isolated wood at dusk, he'd tripped-off a spring alarm gun and been 'arrested' as a poacher by his own keepers!

The duchess was equally delightful, and we soon discovered our common love of dogs. Wherever she went, she was shadowed by her faithful sheep dog 'Collie', which looked a useful type to me, so I asked her if he was any good. 'Any good!' she said. 'Any good! Of course he's good. He's the pride of my life.' 'Will he work sheep, was what I meant,' I said. 'He's quite good,' she said. 'I often use him with my flock of Jacob sheep.'

'What about doing a bit, for the programme?' I asked, putting her on rather an unfair spot. 'Is that a challenge?' she demanded, and I told her it was. 'You're in business then,' she replied, and she proceeded to give an extremely competent demonstration, which endeared her to friend and stranger alike.

Top sheep dog trials had very often been held at Chatsworth, long before we came on the scene, so that many of our competitors had known the Devonshires personally for years and the easy relationship and courteous, friendly familiarity between hosts and guests and owners and tenants and employees would have been an object lesson to petty politicians and commentators who are forever knocking at such scions of society.

Perhaps a common love of dogs and their achievements demolishes the artificial but traditional barriers. Perhaps, when it is possible to escape deep into the wonderful countryside, where we are privileged to record our programme, synthetic differences are cut down to size so that real men (and women!) closely involved with intelligent working dogs achieve their true perspective.

# 4
# ... and his dog

ERIC HALSALL often tells me that 'sheep dogs are the wisest dogs on earth' but that is precisely what the owner of every family pooch would claim for his own dog. I know I would, though that is not to detract from the brilliance of dogs trained to the pitch of winning trials.

Casual viewers often assume, when they see a physically attractive, perfectly trained collie, 'gentling' sheep around a trials course, that he would make the perfect five-star ovine nanny, in whose charge the most vulnerable lamb would be eternally safe.

Nothing is further from the truth. A collie's natural instinct is not to regard sheep as little darlings, to be cosseted, so much as potential lamb chops, to be relished in the mind. Collies are instinctive hunting dogs, and their role as shepherds of the flock has been produced by generations of selective breeding, honed to perfection by training devised by skilful shepherds.

All that is necessary to appreciate this is to watch television programmes about wolves, hunting moose or elk or wild dogs hunting deer on the plains of Africa. The natural canine instinct is to hustle a group of quarry before the pack, until a weakling falters and lags behind, leaving a gap between it and its fellows. When the predators spot this, they dive in and split the laggard from its fellows, separating it until they can close in and kill it.

Now watch a sophisticated collie and his master 'shedding' sheep in a trial. The dog has brought the whole bunch round the course, eventually driving them to his master in the shedding ring, bounded and identified by piles of sawdust.

The shepherd stands firm at the edge of the ring, bringing the sheep

86

*A good shed. All sheep are inside the sawdust ring and the dog has split off the one with the red collar.*

to a halt in a bunch before him. He drops the dog a few yards on the far side of the bunch which, feeling trapped between master and dog, feel uneasy and look for some way of escape. The slightest gesture from the shepherd causes the sheep to stretch out in a line, looking for a safe gap, through which to make a dash.

One sheep has been fitted with a red collar, to denote that the judges have selected it to be the sheep to be 'singled' or separated from her fellows, thus proving that the shepherd and his dog so dominate the sheep that they can not only split, or 'shed', a sheep from her fellows, but any sheep which is selected.

It is an operation which demands not only skill but infinite patience, because it is useless to try to shed the selected sheep until she is not only at one end of the bunch, but has a gap between her and her fellows, through which the dog can be called to make her explode one way and the rest of the bunch in the opposite direction.

If the sheep line out but are drifting towards the edge of the shedding ring, with the red-collared ewe in the middle of the bunch, the drift must be reversed to make a fresh start.

If the dog gets impatient and inches in too close, he will 'spook' the sheep and cause them to bunch even closer for mutual protection. Instinct tells them that isolation from their fellows is their greatest danger. If the man loses his cool and tries to force the issue, there is danger of a spontaneous break for safer pastures. Patience is the key word, and the sheep must be gentled, first in one direction and then in another, until, at last, a red-collared ewe is at one end of the line, with a space between her and her fellows who, ideally, will be facing in the opposite direction.

Repeated experiences of the manoeuvre of the operation enable man and dog to increase the growing gap. The dog will have ears cocked, eyes concentrating and tongue licking chops at the prospect of being called into the gap, to shed the victim from her fellows.

Watch the dog closely, at this instant, when his defences are down, and the naked instinct to drive quarry and split off a weakling is as obvious as it is when the television camera catches wolves performing precisely the same ritual. The only difference is that the wolves eat their quarry while generations of selective breeding and sophisticated training have robbed the sheep dog of his orgasm so that he has to make do with a laconic 'That'll do', which is the nearest thing to enthusistic praise he will hear from his master!

Once having appreciated the significance of the relationship between man and dog, it will become equally obvious that, from the outrun, to get behind the quarry, through the intricate controls on driving through and round obstacles to the climax of penning, trials have as much to do with hunting as stockmanship.

That is part of the reason why the collies in our programme so obviously love their work, which seems less like work to them than pleasure as keen as a terrier hunting rats.

A yardstick of the criteria used in selecting dams and sires of any breed of dog is the behaviour of a litter of puppies which have not yet been weaned.

Play, in young wild animals, is a natural rehearsal of their role when they grow up. A litter of kittens will chase anything that moves, from a table-tennis ball to a feather in the wind. They pounce and immobilise such insensate objects, as they will one day immobilise mice or young rabbits, or birds.

*Stars of tomorrow.*

Young deer in our wood appear to be dozing, one second, and the next they are making mad dashes at full speed among the trees. Although an occasional one misjudges distance and comes to grief by hitting a tree trunk full-tilt, such accidents are rare. The purpose of the exercise, though the deer are doubtless unaware of it, is to 'learn' every snag and obstacle in home territory, so that if, in times to come, a predator appears to give lethal chase, the quarry will know every inch so well that anything which hunts them will be in more danger than its intended victim.

Young spaniels 'naturally' retrieve and are never happier than when bringing a ball or sock or dummy bird to their owner, as one day they will retrieve real quarry in the shooting field.

A litter of sheep dog puppies, left to amuse themselves, will not try to outrun each other, as whippets might, or engage in mock battles, as bull terriers do. Sheep dogs will try to round each other up, at eight or ten weeks old, as they will shepherd sheep when they grow up.

Puppies are always appealing, and film of unweaned whelps stalking each other, each trying to outstare his brother, with mock round-ups as purposeful as champions in a sheep dog trial, cannot fail to top the ratings. The letters we receive when we show such juvenile dramas leave no doubt where our viewers' hearts are.

As the pups grow up, they turn by instinct to any quarry which will retreat before them. There is no peace for free range farmyard ducks and hens, which are rounded up and huddled in a corner, where some precocious pup stretches full length, head on forefeet, daring its quarry to make a break for freedom.

They have the life of Riley for a while, with freedom of the farm, but it soon becomes obvious that the one thing sheep dogs love, above all others, is not unfettered liberty but the discipline of accompanying the boss when he is caring for livestock on the farm.

Shepherds, especially hill shepherds, who cannot count their sheep by leaning over the nearest five-barred gate, spend hours walking wild sheepwalks where their flocks are grazing.

They take the old dogs with them, partly because, like me, they feel half dressed without a favourite dog, but partly for the practical reason that, without a working sheep dog, so many of their sheep will be hidden in gullies or deep cover that there would be no way of knowing whether they are sick or well.

Such dogs do not spend much time meekly walking to heel. They may be anything up to half a mile away, winkling their quarry from concealment, for inspection, sometimes in response to the shepherd's commands, sometimes on their own initiative.

No time is happier for a pup than when he is old enough for promotion to such excursions. He will be required to keep a low profile and walk to heel for quite a while, watching – and envying – his elders and betters at what will be his pride, too, in times to come.

The miles covered by a man in a day on such excursions, literally up hill and down dale, would make hobby hill walkers wince at the prospect. Working dogs multiply this many times, often over loose scree, which is cruel hard on pads, so that the youngsters, even while walking to heel, acquire taut muscles, with little spare flesh and not an ounce of flab. When they are eventually upgraded, to work with the dogs, they join a class which would rival packs of foxhounds or the horses which accompany them.

There are great differences in the ages at which collies show much interest in sheep, just as some guard dogs will bark at strangers before they are weaned, while others are still 'soft as a mop' at twelve months.

Some collies are 'naturals' and will fetch sheep at less than four months old. 'Fetching', to a master (or pack leader), is a natural instinct of many dogs, as anyone with a puppy which positively insists on retrieving a ball, or almost anything portable, will know. In collies, it is partly the result of good stockmanship, which has ensured that the best performers in many generations have been selected as dams and sires, deliberately 'fixing' required points. It is also partly instinct which dips back to the basic origins of canine behaviour.

Not much specific training can be done until the young dog does indicate an interest in sheep, when one of the first steps is to send him out, on easy runs, to fetch a bunch of sheep he can see, when the first command will be a verbal 'shoosh' (which excites almost all dogs), or a whistle command, which will not have to be repeated many times before the dog understands it to mean 'walk on' – or go straight ahead.

Serious training can rarely begin at much less than eight or ten months old, though young puppies will learn, for the price of a tit-bit as bribe, to come when called and sit or lie when told. Provided such lessons are made fun and not a chore, demonstrative praise will soon be as effective as the tit-bit.

A common ploy is for the shepherd to put a bunch of docile, well handled sheep in a small enclosure, just in case(!) the young dog gets too enthusiastic. The shepherd can then get to close quarters, to nip trouble in the bud, instead of seeing dog and sheep disappearing over the horizon, as could happen in encounters in open hill country. The dog, perhaps more by accident than design initially, will drive his sheep towards the shepherd, who will encourage him to bring them as close to his feet as possible. This will not be what the sheep have in mind, so that, sooner or later, one will make a break for it.

Feeling on top of the world with his achievement of 'presenting' the sheep to the boss, the dog may hang back, and head the fugitive back to the bunch, like an old hand at the game. But it is far more likely that he will lose his cool and rush in to grab – or 'grip' – the rebel, as the wild hunting dogs in his ancestry would have done.

Although 'gripping' is a cardinal sin, in a trials dog, for which he can be excluded from the trial, it is a perfectly natural instinct which it is wise to tolerate at the early stage of training, lest a reprimand is misunderstood by the dog, who may take it that any contact with sheep is forbidden.

Having rounded-up his quarry successfully, and brought it to his pack leader, the shepherd – getting extremely excited in the process, it is instinctive to restrain a victim, trying a last minute escape, even if it involves biting or 'gripping' it to instil the necessary discipline.

91

*A 'ladder style' is built over a wall so that spectators can come and go as they wish, hidden from cameras by the wall.*

*The finished ladder-style.*

The vital thing, at this stage of training, is not to daunt the young dog by punishing him for something he does not know is wrong.

The obvious objection that being 'gripped' must be pretty unpleasant for the sheep is not serious either, because normal gripping – as opposed to naked savaging, which would never be tolerated – amounts to little more than holding the sheep by its fleece without penetrating down to the flesh.

In time to come, when the trained dog is worked on the farm, as opposed to performing on the trials field, it may be vital that he is prepared to grip.

Ewes, lambing out on the hill, may have to be caught by the shepherd and handled while he gives treatment for some problem before or while giving birth. A dog which will go in, on command, and grip the selected ewe, 'throwing' her on her back, as a wrestler would, if necessary, until his master can get close enough to handle her himself, is an essential tool of the trade.

A stroppy old ewe can be a formidable opponent for any dog at lambing time, and the only way of disciplining her may be to allow the dog to establish supremacy, once and for all, by putting her in her place the hard way.

The capacity to do so may literally be a matter of life or death to the dog, because if the flock is brought down to the farmstead, to lamb, it will be under cover, in a sheepyard, or confined by the walls of a small paddock. Ewes, at this time, are fiercely protective of their newborn lambs, and quite prepared to lower their heads to charge at any interloping dog. If they do so, they may trap the dog between their battering ram of a skull and the solid wall of the yard or paddock. Many a good dog has been killed in such a charge.

The reason that this rarely happens to top class dogs, with professional shepherds, is that the risk is known, and the dog not only allowed but encouraged to charge first and establish supremacy by gripping the threatening ewe.

Among the most irresponsible advice I ever heard on television was a pundit telling rural fugitives from towns how to prevent their ill-disciplined dogs from sheep worrying.

'Take Fido to the nearest sheep farmer,' the oaf said, 'and ask him to let you shut the dog in a loosebox with a newly lambed ewe. She will teach him a lesson.' She surely would. Before the poor pooch knew what had hit him, the chances are that he would be flattened against the wall and crippled, if not killed.

93

It is important, therefore, not to sneap, or cow, a puppy which is just beginning to enjoy shepherding sheep, simply because he gets a bit over-exuberant and grips. There is time enough to tone him down, so that he never offends in this respect without an invitation.

The basics of subsequent training are simple, although the man and dog will continue to build on the framework by absorbing experience for years to come. A trials dog will not be at his best until four or five years old. By that time the phizz will have gone off and he will have tempered exuberance by experience, so that he will be able to forecast the ploys of cunning sheep, taking them precisely where the shepherd wants, smoothly and directly.

The basic commands for this are astonishingly simple, because the whole operation can be concluded by using only four commands. They are Walk On, Go Right, Go Left, or Stop. To embellish the mystique, most shepherds 'Away to me,' when they mean Go Right, 'Come bye,' when they mean Go Left, and 'Stand' when they mean either Go Slow or Stop. Most specialist pastimes are punctuated by such foibles.

To comprehend how this is done, it is only necessary to visualise a trial. The shepherd and his dog come to the starting post and the man settles his dog either on his right or left side, depending upon which side he wants the dog to take for his outrun. Being perfectly aware of the pleasures to come, the dog scans the horizon for his sheep and the shepherd assures himself that the dog has spotted the right sheep, when the release pen shepherds have driven them towards the lift post.

When he is given permission to commence the trial, all that would be necessary would be for the shepherd to give the command Walk On. He normally 'shooshes' the dog away instead, because that is a sound that excites all dogs, so that the dog does not walk on but dashes on, giving his performance more polish and sparkle.

The natural instinct of the dog – prompted, if necessary, by the shepherd – is to take an outrun in a direction which will not startle the sheep by going directly towards them or passing too close. His instinct is to run in an arc which will take him wide but curve round behind them so that the first they will know is when the dog appears behind them, putting them directly between the dog, within a few yards, and his master, a quarter of a mile or more away.

The second command 'Stop' is now used, usually by whistle, and the dog will stop and wait instructions, though the sheep will obviously register his presence.

94

When the shepherd blows 'Walk On,' to start the dog towards the sheep, he will 'lift' them and they will move off in the general direction of the shepherd, beginning the Fetch leg of the trial.

Sod's Law decrees that if anything can go wrong, it will, so the bunch of sheep will not go directly to, and through the Fetch gate, if left to their own devices. They will veer, instead, either to the right or left. In order to correct this deviation, it is necessary to make the dog follow, or ideally, anticipate this, and move over behind them to drive them back to their straight and narrow line. So he blows his Go Right or Go Left command, as necessary, to correct them.

If they go too fast he will order the dog to stand, usually by a single, insistent whistle blast, and, if they dawdle and graze, he orders the dog to Walk On, to liven them up a bit.

When the bunch of sheep have been brought from the lift and through the Fetch gates, the dog has to turn them, as tightly as possible round the shepherd, and then take them away from him, on the Drive Away. It is perfectly natural for the dog to bring the sheep to his handler. From the canine point of view, it is not natural to drive such valuable possessions away again! He must think that the boss has gone bonkers and can't make up his mind what he does want!

Nevertheless, the manoeuvre is completed by what the dog must feel to be mindless obedience to commands he has rehearsed so often that compliance has become a reflex.

The sheep will come through the Fetch gate down to the right hand side of the shepherd and, the moment they pass him, he will give the command to put his dog diagonally across them, making them turn towards the Drive Away gate and on to the cross drive.

If they deviate, the dog will be sent right or left, just enough to correct, but not to over-correct, the error. If they slow, the command Walk On will persuade them to change gear. If they go too fast, the Stop whistle will lengthen the space between them and their pursuer, so that they will feel they can safely ease up.

The great danger is stampeding them too fast downhill, for sheep do not have good brakes and are likely to fetch up in the car park or over the horizon, to the embarrassment of both man and dog.

Having been gentled smoothly round the course, the sheep are brought into the sawdust shedding ring, where one of the two wearing red collars must be shed, or split off from her fellows, and 'worn' – or kept split off – until the judges give the word that they are satisfied the dog is totally in command.

7

5

6

1 *Dog by shepherd, ready for outrun which will begin when the shepherd is satisfied he has seen the bunch of sheep at top of the field.*

2 *Dog goes away on right hand outrun.*

3 *Dog behind his sheep, lifting them and starting the Fetch.*

4, 5, 6, 7 *Various stages of Fetch, coming through Fetch gates. Sheep are brought tight round the shepherd to begin the Drive Away.*

Immense patience is needed as the shepherd makes subtle move-ments with his hands to get the sheep moving, without alarming them.

They can't retreat directly away from him, because the dog, which has bossed them round the course, is positioned on the opposite side of the bunch.

Their easiest (apparent!) way to escape is to stream off, single file, either to right or left, and the shepherd steps back, to lift the threat, or closes in slightly, to motivate them in an effort to persuade them to string out, as widely as possible, in single file, so that, when the moment comes, he can call in the dog through a gap, to split the bunch in opposite directions.

If any sheep would do, he could call the dog as soon as a wide enough gap appeared between the end sheep in line and her fellows. But any sheep won't do. To demonstrate complete control, the sheep which is eventually shed must be one with a red collar and, on the law of averages, the two red-collared sheep may be some time before one happens to move into a possible place for 'singling'.

The very fact that she is wearing a red collar may aggravate this because the release shepherds will only recently have caught and handled her to fit it, and she may take precautions against being handled again, by burying herself in the middle of the bunch and refusing the more exposed position at the end of the line.

A shepherd who loses his cool will make this worse and, if he grows impatient, he may 'spook' the whole bunch into bolting out of the sawdust shedding ring, where the manoeuvre must be completed. 'Softly, softly, catchee monkey' was never more true than in the shedding ring, and the top competitors are never bounced into taking unrealistic chances.

Dogs, which are hunting predators, geared to run down their prey and separate the weakling, must regard such prevarication by their boss as a feline weakness, fit only for cats, which waste endless hours before pouncing on a mouse.

This becomes obvious on the box as the crouching collie shivers with excitement, licking his lips in anticipation, flashing eyes pleading for the command 'Come Through,' which is simply the dramatic version of Walk On, changed from command to invitation.

Penning, the last phase of our Singles Trial, simply consists of putting the whole bunch inside a small hurdle pen made so that the hurdle forming the fourth side can be swung-to by the competitor, holding a rope fixed to the hurdle which is hinged at one end.

*Sheep being fitted with red collars. One of these must be separated in trial in 'shedding ring' to demonstrate control. One of these collars is fitted with radio mike to give sound effects of sheep going over the course.*

This is not as simple as it looks, if only because the pen is erected in the middle of such a large open space that there seems all the room in the world for the sheep to go round it, instead of submitting to the obvious risks of incarceration inside!

So, after shedding, the shepherd walks over to the pen, opens the swinging hurdle and holds the other end of the rope attached to it, so that he makes one side of a funnel, designed to guide the sheep into captivity at the end of the trial.

The dog brings them towards the pen, flanking the unguarded side, hopefully to form the other side of the funnel, formed by the open gate, rope and shepherd.

There is often a stroppy old ewe in the bunch which decides that such captivity is not for her, however docile and co-operative her weaker-minded fellows may be. So she turns round, to face the dog, lowers her head and stamps a forefoot.

The reactions of dogs to this threat display are fascinating and varied. Some dogs, which are gentle and kind will avert their gaze in a gesture of instinctive canine submission. It may simply be that they

99

(Opposite above) *Sheep brought to within an ace of the final pen.*

(Opposite centre) *They mutiny and break away.*

(Opposite below) *Dog sent wide to bring them back.*

(Above top) *Nicely back, with shepherd holding swinging gate by rope one side and dog blocking escape the other.*

(Above bottom) *Got 'em. Shepherd swings gate shut behind them.*

are submissive, by nature, and possibly exceptionally easy to train in consequence. Or it may be that, in the past, a highly protective old ewe has charged them and smashed them against a wall in protection of her lamb. Whatever the cause, it becomes a battle of wills between a dominant and dangerous ewe and the dog, which is proving his worth by driving her and her fellows into captivity.

Strong, bold dogs will meet the challenge and, in the privacy of their own farms, would probably be allowed to assert their authority by 'gripping' the mutinous ewe and putting her in her place. Thereafter she would treat the dog with due respect and indulge in no more trials of strength!

This cannot be allowed to happen at a trial, where the dog would be disqualified for gripping, so that the contest becomes a battle of wills instead of physical strength.

So, at the beginning of a trial, very soon after the outrun, when the dog is behind his sheep, ready to 'lift' and 'fetch' them, it is often possible to watch the drama, as they get the feel of each other and establish their relative levels.

This is where the dog's 'eye' comes in. Much of the canine-sheep relationship is a matter of sheer willpower, transmitted through the eyes. The dog stares at his sheep and the glowering threats in his eyes are translated into tangible exercise of canine fangs in the sheep's mind. A really 'strong eyed' dog rarely has his bluff called – because the chances are it isn't bluff!

The 'strength of eye' in successful, dominant collies is partly instinctive threat-display, but partly a symptom of intense concentration, similar to the concentration of a pointer or setter engaged in finding game, hidden in deep cover.

There is a strong tradition in the sheep dog world that a cross of setter was introduced to collie blood, specifically to breed 'strong eyed' dogs which would be capable of subduing the most arrogant sheep by the intensity of their threatening stare.

Watching sheep dogs, it is often possible to visualise sporting setters or pointers in their place. Having come up to their quarry they freeze as rigid as a sporting setter which knows that the grouse it has winded lies motionless a few yards in front of its nose, concealed from view in the centre of a clump of heather but nakedly exposed to the most sophisticated sense of smell.

Therein lies a snag. When the guns have caught up and are well within range of their pointing dog, they wish to send the dog in to flush the bird so that they can shoot it. Such is the rigid concentration of the dog that he will sometimes be frozen in his tracks, so immobilised by his one-track mind that the sportsman finds it impossible to persuade him to dash in to flush his quarry to the guns when they are ready to fire a broadside.

The same sometimes happens with collies. The sheep are manoeuvred to within an ace of victory, but the dog becomes so intoxicated by his achievement that he remains rooted to the spot, instead of jumping to the command to dive in and shed off a red collar or gentle the last potential rebel safely into the pen.

So it is not only essential to breed dogs with sufficient hereditary dominance to convince their sheep of the futility of resistance, but also to give them so much experience of success that it never crosses their minds that they will not triumph over the most bloody-minded ewe.

There is, of course, one practice that is even more potentially danger-ous than putting a dog in a position where he may be splattered on the wall by the irresistible charge of a ewe protecting her lamb or by

*A heifer can be very forbidding.*

an aggressive tup. The job of cattle dog is particular dangerous, not only from the horns of charging cows, but from their hooves as well.

A bunch of driven cattle may appear to be pretty harmless unless the dog actually gets in front of them and is gored or trodden underfoot if they stampede.

But, pushing the laggards along, a dog is always liable to stop a wicked side-kick as tail-end Sally lashes out in protest that Time is her servant, not her master, and that no dog will harry her with impunity. The horny cloven rear hooves of cattle are lethal weapons which will gouge out a dog's eye, break a limb or jaw, or inflict horrific gashes.

The Welsh bred short-legged corgis, which are known as 'heelers', are supposed to be able to nip the heels of cattle, to hurry them on with impunity, immune from retaliation because they are so low to the ground that swipes from hind feet are supposed to pass harmlessly over their heads.

Having no practical experience with corgis, I am unable to vouch for such miraculous escapes from retribution, but there is no doubt that a great many Border collies have been crippled and ruined by cattle.

Plenty of hill farmers, who run both sheep and cattle on their ground, marshal both with collies which seem to come to no harm. If the dog is lucky enough to sustain a few relatively minor buffets early in his career, he will learn from experience the wisdom of keeping out of range of spiteful hooves.

Once they have established their relative levels, the cattle will accept the inevitable, that the dog is master. He will need to have been a strong and aggressive dog to have got so far though, and may become as addicted to violence as urban human thugs so that it will be difficult to persuade him not to bully sheep.

Suckler cows, with calves at foot, are even more dangerous because they will charge and trample dogs, as well as kicking at them, if they have the chance.

So most collies run in sheep dog trials are, as the term suggests, specialists on sheep, the 'strong' dogs dominating them, and very gentle, kind dogs sometimes proving ineffective, even with sheep, if they come up against real opposition.

No two are the same, so that every trial poses different problems. The permutations of different sheep and dogs and men, and conditions in which they compete, are infinite.

The more trials one watches the more fascinating it becomes to discover precisely how such problems are solved. It soon becomes more and more obvious that a dog trained to such a pitch of obedience that he becomes an automaton will be beaten by a rival which has been left some latitude to think for himself.

Raymond Macpherson is widely acclaimed as being amongst the finest competing shepherds in the world and he ran his dog Tweed in our trials at Bala in North Wales. It was a particularly testing competition because, instead of the *whole* course being in view of competitors and spectators, as it is at more conventional trials, the Fetch entailed bringing sheep out of sight, behind some trees, at right angles to the shepherd, who could see neither sheep nor his dog as they moved for some distance shielded by cover. He could give voice or whistle commands to the dog – but there was no way he could see if he was complying.

This of course, is an everyday occurrence at home when the dogs are working sheep amongst bracken or scrub or heather on the hill but it does not normally happen in trials where viewers can see it all on the screen – and criticise!

After the sheep had been driven some distance out of sight, they came to a gap through which the competitor was required to get his dog to bring them across a stream, down towards him.

All seemed to be going to plan and, when the sheep appeared at the gap, Raymond gave his dog the command to bring them on down to him.

Despite being a dog of top International class, Tweed flatly refused to come a step through the gap.

Raymond whistled him on but the dog stood irresolute. He shouted at him but still with no result. Such defiance is unheard of at such levels of perfection and only when real anger tainted the words with threats did the dog submit and consent to start to drive his sheep on towards his master.

Then the truth dawned, first on Raymond and then on knowledgeable spectators, that the dog was right and he was wrong! Tweed's reluctance to come on had been prompted by reason, not insolence. Although his boss hadn't noticed it, one sheep had slipped away from her fellows while out of sight and hived-up in cover.

Tweed knew this, which was why he wouldn't come with an incomplete packet of sheep onto the field and his stance at the gap had been a plea to be allowed to return and retrieve the truant.

When he unwillingly complied with stern commands to stop messing about and come on it resulted in the sheep minus one being driven out into the open and, if they had continued, Raymond would have been disqualified.

He was too wise a bird for that. When he subconsciously counted his sheep and found one short he did not panic, whatever shock it gave him.

If he had sent the dog straight back through the gap to find the truant he might have panicked it away to the middle distance and made matters worse so he simply gave the command to stop and made the dog lie down where he was.

The pressure off, the sheep settled down to graze between the gap in the hedge and the next obstacle.

Sheep are by nature flock animals and don't like being alone in strange places so that the truant lost the courage of her convictions and, wondering where her fellows had gone, came tentatively to the gap and peered through. Seeing that the rest were quietly grazing, she immediately wandered down, of her own accord, to join them, as Raymond had obviously predicted. He allowed her to come on down till there was safe room to send Tweed to cut her off if she changed her mind about the delights of escape – and brought the whole bunch on as if nothing untoward had happened.

He was of course penalised for the mistake – but not disqualified, as he would have been if he had continued with an incomplete bunch of sheep.

But the episode proved that Eric is right when he says that 'sheep dogs are among the wisest dogs on earth'. After watching such an episode, who can doubt that they are *not* the well trained automatons some would have us believe. They are most certainly capable of constructive thought and brave enough to defy the master who has trained them to such a state of perfection *when* they are certain that they are right and he is wrong!

However much boffins, superglued to laboratory stools, may scoff at the idea of putting constructive thought into the head of a dog, there is no shadow of doubt, in my mind, that it took great mental courage for Tweed to defy a master he loved and respected, to refuse repeated commands to come on through to drive six sheep, when he knew he should have had seven. I make no apology for being anthropomorphic enough to believe the dog was so convinced that he was right and the boss was wrong that his insubordination was justified. It was also superb television!

106

Brace trials are among the most sophisticated and engrossing spectacles of any form of sheep dog competition. The competitor is required to work two dogs, at the same time, which must work in unison, each taking an equal share in bringing the sheep round the course.

They have an extremely practical application in real life, because when hundreds, rather than dozens, of sheep have to be controlled and gathered in hostile habitat, the best dog in the world couldn't cope on his own.

In practice, at home, when a complicated gather has to be performed, over thousands of acres of mountainside, it is customary to ask neighbours to help – and bring their own dogs. It is not uncommon to see a dozen or so men, with a dog or two apiece, spread out as far as eye can see over the hills.

For competition purposes, the skills are distilled down, not to one man and his dog – but to one man and two dogs.

The outrun is fairly simple, with one dog taking the right flank outrun, and the other the left, so that they converge behind the sheep in swinging arcs, from each side. One dog may be older and much slower than his partner so that, to make a spectacular two-sided gather, the shepherd has to start the slower dog first to ensure that they arrive behind the sheep simultaneously. If they cross, at the apex of their outrun, they must stay on the flank to which they crossed

*Dog driving sheep away on cross drive.*

over, as changing from one side to the other is permitted only once in each trial.

When they get the command Walk On, either verbal or by whistle, they must 'lift' the sheep and bring them down to the Fetch gate, one dog driving from each side. To correct any deviation from the straight line by the sheep, it will need one dog holding back and the other pushing. This obviously requires a different command for each dog because if, for example, they had both been trained to Go Right in response to the same notes on the whistle, both dogs would go right or left or stop or start, or stop simultaneously, instead of each dog reacting differently, as the shepherd wished.

So the ultimate sophistication of brace work is that each dog must be trained individually, to obey commands meant for him but to ignore commands meant for his partner. Each dog has to be trained to his own individual whistle commands, which the other dog must ignore, and I have watched Glyn Jones, a Welsh shepherd with an English wife, giving instructions to one dog of his brace in English while speaking to the other dog in Welsh!

This provides a complicated mental juggling act, where the competitor controls his two dogs, several hundred yards away, so that they stop and start and weave, from side to side, keeping the flow of sheep in a straight line, from the centre of each obstacle to the centre of the next.

Instead of shedding a sheep with a red collar, a larger bunch of sheep has to be divided in halves – 'split down the middle', as Eric puts it – and one bunch penned in a three-sided pen, without the normal fourth side that acts as a gate, by one dog, which then has to lie down in the opening, and concentrate on his captives, to prevent them escaping and joining up with their free fellows, which they will do if given half a chance.

Meanwhile, the other dog is expected to 'wear' his bunch and keep them well out of the way, while the first half is being penned in the three-sided pen.

The next act in the drama is for the first dog to be left, unsupervised, while the shepherd walks over to the second pen, which has the conventional three sides and swinging gate, where the other dog is expected to pen the remainder of the original batch of sheep.

Barring accidents, this may be fairly easy, but if the sheep are stroppy and try to rejoin their fellows in the first pen, or otherwise play up, the temptations to the first dog are almost irresistible. It will seem wrong, to him, to sit on his backside by a pen, where the sheep have already been penned, while his partner is so obviously in difficulties – and while his attention is diverted, as he watches events across the trials field, his own charges may take advantage of his lapse and make a bid for escape, in which case the competitor will be required to do the first pen all over again or, if they actually manage to merge, the trial will go back to the shedding stage.

To add to such complications, one dog is sometimes jealous of his partner, who he regards more as a rival than a partner, so that the shepherd's natural difficulties with rebellious sheep are compounded by clashes of canine psychology. The more such mental duels I watch, the deeper my appreciation of the finer points of the sport. Such incidents really do separate the men from the boys amongst the competitors, so that I believe it is no coincidence that the really old stagers not only have dogs which obey them implicitly, ninety-nine per cent of the time, but also think for themselves by anticipating problems.

The late Dick Fortune was just such a character, and his run with his old bitch Jill at Austwick, in North Yorkshire, will always stick in my mind.

It was an unusual course because two of the 'gates', through which the sheep had to be driven, were not conventional hurdles, erected like thumbs in a desert, with space on either side of them. They were gaps in a dour grey stone wall which bisected the course, and the dog had to pass through one, to collect unseen sheep, and bring them down, through another, to the shedding ring.

On her first run, Jill gentled the sheep to the correct gap, in fine style, but as soon as they emerged into the unknown, on the spectators' side, they exploded and bolted downhill, in the wrong direction, though Dick and his bitch eventually retrieved the situation and won the round.

Realising that the bossy old ewe in the next round might lead her little flock astray by playing a similar prank, Jill was obviously determined to forestall them.

She gentled them through the gap and, sure enough, they began to veer off course – but their caper was cut off at source. Instead of following them through the gap, the old bitch dashed off downhill, out of their sight, behind the wall, jumped over, about fifty yards below them, so that they caame unexpectedly face to face with their pursuer, who they had imagined was in the next field. She made her point that she was boss, so they conceded victory and behaved impeccably for the rest of the round.

Such dogs may, indeed, be born through generations of selective breeding by clever stockmen, but they are also made by 'naturals' like Dick Fortune.

He started his working life shepherding in East Lothian, in Scotland, but in the Great Depression in the 1930s he packed his bags and departed for New Zealand, where he found his true level and ended up with a successful sheep ranch of two and a half thousand acres, importing a hundred collies from England, while he was there, with which he gave exhibitions and convinced the New Zealanders that a good collie is worth his weight in gold on any farm.

When he retired and came 'home' he settled near Edinburgh, but he was so addicted to sheep dogs that he couldn't break the habit, and I shall never forget the cameos, at Dick's home, when the old boy was training his dog, not on some wild and picturesque farm in the hills, but in the incongruous setting of the paddock of a bungalow on the outskirts of a great city.

The old boy, like most real characters, was a great extrovert, and he was smartly dressed, sitting on a stump in the centre of his oasis of green, in the urban desert, working a bunch of sheep this way and that, in his postage stamp field, as unselfconsciously as if he'd been in the outback of New Zealand. He kept a few sheep for his dogs to shepherd, rather than dogs to shepherd his sheep, and topped off the eccentric cameo by wearing a wide-brimmed hat, like a stetson.

He now had all the time there was, so that his dedication paid off by producing clever dogs, like Jill, who rewarded his patience by using the latitude he gave her to think, as well as to obey.

Examples like that still do not convince the boffins, who say that dogs work purely by instinct, tempered by the sort of Pavlovian training which deliberately mixes cruelty with kindness, but anyone who is really involved with working dogs can give the lie to that.

The doors in our house are opened by levers, as opposed to conventional round door knobs, and several of our dogs have discovered, by the accident of standing on hind legs, that if they depress the lever with a front paw, they can push open a door which was previously latched. There is nothing very clever about that, though the more extreme among the boffins seem to think that it normally takes generations of evolution to convert chance experience into practical knowledge.

110

Two of my present dogs, Belle the alsatian and Nip the half-bred alsatian, have taken door-opening a stage further, because they can open our doors either away from them, which is easy, or towards them, which requires more intelligence. They have discovered that, by standing on hind legs and depressing the handle, an inwards-opening door will work if they hook a front paw round the lever and pull instead of push.

Belle has taught herself a far more intricate trick. My study is an addition to the house, so that we lock the back door when we go to bed, and leave Belle and Tarka, the Rottweiler, to sleep in the study with the door open. The open study door allows the dogs to go out into the yard and paddock, which are surrounded by a dog-proof fence and contain the garage, tractor shed and hen pen. If the dogs hear any intruder after we have gone to bed, they are free to patrol half an acre or a little more round two sides of the house – which does little for the confidence of uninvited guests!

For some reason, which I have not been able to fathom, Belle decided, after twelve years sleeping in the study, that she would prefer to sleep in my car, where I found her on the back seat one morning. Thinking that I must have left the door open, I checked that it was latched next night – but she was on the back seat again next morning.

Women passengers get rather narrow minded if their car seat is plastered with mud off the feet of dogs which have checked every inch of a muddy yard and grassy paddock is free of intruders before they retire, so I took steps to deter her. I simply locked the car door, leaving the key in the lock for convenience.

Next day the key was on the floor, and there were scratches round the handle, as clues to an unsuccessful attempt at burglary. I decided to outwit her once and for all, establishing that canine intelligence is no match for mine.

When she returned the next night she got a shock! I had attached the lead of an electric fencing unit to the chassis. The rubber tyres insulated the car so that anyone touching bare metal received a slight shock, which did them no harm, but just such a small reminder is all that is needed to stop sheep and cattle straying. She took the hint, so that, next morning, Belle was back in the study.

My victory was short-lived. It lasted no more than a night. The following morning, Belle was back in the car, despite the fact that the chassis was 'alive'. I discovered that the plastic handle was held on by two bolts, one at each side, and that if I put a finger on either of these,

I got a mild shock. But, using extreme care, it was just possible to grasp the plastic, between the bolts, and lift the handle to open the door without touching bare metal.

Belle had cracked the problem and, in one night, she had learned to grasp the only section of the door handle which would allow her to retire to her chosen couch without suffering even minor discomfort. Houdini had nothing on her, so I accepted my defeat gracefully, and any females who object are more than welcome to walk!

Most people who are deeply attached to their dogs could tell anecdotes about the sagacity which has filled their lives with similar incidents. One of the main attractions of watching *One Man and His Dog* is that it provides an opportunity of rubbing shoulders with men and women with similar tastes, and watching dogs with different skills from theirs.

People often ask me why only Border collies are run in sheep dog trials. Why not other breeds? The simple answer is that no other breed of dog is as good as a Border collie at the job. Some breeds have been ruined by the dog-showing fraternity, which selects dams and sires for their cosmetic appearance rather than for their ability to shepherd sheep.

Selective breeding is, of necessity, a matter of compromise, since no animal is perfect. An animal which has most of the qualities required is likely to lack others or, worse still, carry a hereditary gene which is a positive disadvantage.

Bulldogs are perhaps the best (or worst!) example of such faulty selection. They were originally produced for the barbarous 'sport'(!) of baiting bulls, which demanded great strength and courage. The most successful dogs had short jaws, to give great leverage when they laid hold, and laid-back nostrils so that they could continue to breathe while hanging on, without the danger that the flesh of their victim would overlap their jaws and stifle them.

Bull baiting was eventually outlawed, not as it happens because it was so cruel but because it attracted riotous assemblies, as football does today. So bulldogs, no longer actively used, continued to be bred for show, where foolish exhibitors deliberately exaggerated features suggesting strength and courage and tenacity. The poor caricatures which now waddle round in dog shows are so barrel-chested and squat that toads are things of beauty by comparison. Their nostrils are so laid back that asthma is a common complaint of the breed, and their heads are so large that many bitches find it impossible to produce

112

whelps by natural birth so that Caesarian operations are common.

Many of our large breeds, approved by the Kennel Club, have a high incidence of hip dysplasia and are useless for any activity more strenuous that poncing round a show ring on the end of a lead and, when the judge wishes to assess their profile, sycophantic owners kneel reverently on one knee, holding the tail of their pooch up, with one hand, and his head with the other.

Even with a purely working breed, like Border collies, there are great dangers involved in selective breeding, though shepherds, who value deeds more than looks, have found the answer.

A generation or so ago, it happened that some of the very best working dogs were suffering from a hereditary eye disease known as Progressive Retinal Atrophy, or PRA.

The dog's eyes appeared perfectly normal for the first twelve months or so, after which the field of vision gradually narrowed with age until, by about the age of eight, he had 'tunnel' vision which allowed him to see perfectly well – but only in a progressively narrowing tunnel, or band, which eventually closed in and rendered him blind. This did not usually occur until he was eight or nine years old, by which time his useful working life, in any case, was drawing to a close.

Ironically, the disease did not necessarily ruin his performance in sheep dog trials until his speed had fallen off enough for him to be surpassed by younger, faster dogs.

While his increasingly 'tunnel' vision was still good in a restricted field, he could stand by the shepherd at the start post and, by panning his head from side to side, he could spot sheep coming out of the holding pen and being driven to the Fetch post. So he knew approximately where they were.

A danger with very experienced collies is that they sometimes think they know what is wanted better than the shepherd does, so that they may use too much rather than too little initiative.

A dog losing his sight through progressive retinal atrophy is forced to be more and more dependent on his master for second-by-second instructions, so that the sheep are handled precisely according to instructions, without any canine 'good ideas' to interfere with them.

The result was that dogs so afflicted were tolerated and, because some of them were exceptionally successful, many such winners were used as sires. By the 1970s, up to about thirty per cent of trials dogs carried the gene for Progressive Retinal Atrophy, which could only have got worse if no action had been taken.

Fortunately, the International Sheep Dog Society, the governing body of the sport, was willing to take action, and their decision coincided with research on the subject carried out by Dr Keith Barnett, a world expert on canine sight, so it was agreed that he would examine the eyes of dogs competing at major trials. PRA symptoms can be diagnosed on the spot, after the age of twelve months or so, and younger dogs would not be competing at that level, so it was possible to diagnose the complaint by the time the dogs were experienced enough to have reached top trials status.

The ISDS decreed that dogs not given a clear bill of optical health by Keith Barnett would not be registered by the Society, so that their offspring could not be sold with an official working pedigree.

This had the immediate effect of deflating their value and making them virtually worthless, because they had no 'official' pedigree or papers. It was a far-sighted, bold experiment which has paid off handsomely because the incidence of this insidious disease has fallen from around thirty per cent to three per cent in the decade since it started.

Always willing to pull my leg, someone insisted that Keith examined my eyes – and his diagnosis was that it was hardly worth 'running me on'. I had a narrow escape from the knackers' yard!

How heartening it would be if dog exhibitors would follow the example. If the Kennel Club would decree that show breeds such as German shepherds or labradors, which are so prone to hip dysplasia, or pugs or bulldogs more famous for wheezing respiratory defects than courage or intelligence, could not be registered unless certified free from hereditary disease to which the breed is specially susceptible, show dogs could soon be as healthy – and possibly as intelligent – as breeds which have to rely on deeds not looks for their success.

Not, I fear, that there is much chance of effective action being taken because money is the key, and there are too many dog showers who would lose a fortune if unsound pooches suddenly became worthless.

That, of course, is their business. Those, like me, who do not wish to take the risk of buying a dog bred for show, are not obliged to do so. But unfortunately the matter does not rest there, because there is a great danger that they will 'standardize' Border collies and ruin yet another breed.

Until recently, collies were not 'recognised' for show, largely, I suppose, because there was no official 'standard' by which competing dogs could be compared for excellence in the ring.

Anyone who watches *One Man and His Dog* will see a great variety

114

of collies coming to the trials field. Some like rough-coated dogs which will stand hard weather in winter – but may suffer when required to run many miles up hill and down dale in summer. So there are quite a few top class smooth-coated dogs which meet that requirement.

There are big dogs and quite small ones. Some are flashy black and white, others almost black. Too much white about the head is not favoured because it is very conspicuous in dour fells and may 'spook' the sheep. There have been some excellent red and white dogs, because red and black are common mutations, as any who have bred yellow pups from black labradors, or black-haired children from ginger-headed Irishmen will know. The reason there are not more red and white collies has more to do with their slightly 'foxy' appearance than any defect in their work. With sheep dogs, it is not how pretty they look that counts, but how they do their job.

'Obedience' trials are now a popular pastime, especially in towns, where there is little better to do. Dogs are trained to walk very closely to heel and run through pipes or weave in and out between lines of pegs and jump obstacles, or sit patiently while their boss goes out of sight. It is a flashy exhibition, widely regarded as a load of circus tricks by shepherds or sportsmen who use working dogs in the shooting field.

Until fairly recently, German shepherds were the stars of this 'obedience' work, but it was then discovered that working sheep dogs were even more willing to please and, once trained, they were almost invincible.

Unfortunately, many of these competitions are held at official dog shows, and the organisers of such events apparently insist that any dog competing, in the show ring or elsewhere, must be 'registered' by the Kennel Club.

There was therefore great pressure to have Border collies recognised – and great resistance from many admirers of the breed, against such a move. Those in favour of registration carried the day, and the immediate requirement was for a 'standard' to be drawn up to describe the dogs to be put on file.

How can you draw up a standard for a breed whose only common factor is excellence in herding sheep? Should it be big or small? Long coated or smooth? Black or red? And how much white?

A move was started to hold 'Beauty'(!!) classes, where dogs would compete for purely cosmetic reasons. The 'prettiest' dog would win; whether he would eat a sheep or run away from it would be beside the point.

115

They had a 'beauty' class for German shepherds and the jokesters who formulated that standard thought a dog was 'beautiful' if his back sloped down towards the haunches, and there are those who believe that the prevalence of hip dysplasia in the breed has been in-bred by the type of dog produced to win such so-called beauty classes.

Fortunately the Sheep Dog Trials men will tolerate no such nonsense, and they will continue to select their breeding stock by deeds, not pretty-pretty looks.

The result could be that there may soon be two distinct types of working collie. Those which compete in the trials field, doing to perfection what their ancestors did, will be rough or smooth, long or short coated, with all the rich variety of dogs which have starred on our programme for the last decade. They will be unbeatable on work with sheep.

There will evolve other dogs for a different purpose, either cosmetic dog shows or 'obedience' work, where canine automatons perform as mindlessly as puppets on a string.

This has already happened with some sporting breeds, and there are very few truly dual purpose labrador retrievers, for example, which are champions on the show bench and have also come out top at three Field Trial championships.

The danger is that the selling price of dogs, which has unfortunately inflated partly because of their exposure on the box, will become involved with 'official' paper pedigrees, as has happened for years with dogs produced for shows. The breed could then be split into Pedigree Show Border collies and Working Sheep Dogs which would earn an honest living shepherding sheep and are capable of demonstrating exactly how it is done upon the trials field.

How far such nonsense goes will partly depend on the International Sheep Dog Society, which was formed for the specific purpose of furthering the interests of working collies. Some were surprised that they ever succumbed to having the breed 'recognised' for dog shows, since it is obviously impossible to show dogs competitively without having a specific standard of appearance against which to award points to establish a winner which conformed best to the standard laid down.

Taken to a logical conclusion, some of the best working dogs could be excluded because they have smooth coats, their backs slope too much (or too little!), or they were the 'wrong' colour. As with horses, 'no good dog is a bad colour', in the eyes of real stockmen.

'Shepherding' dogs, of course, were not all evolved for their ability to collect sheep from the great open spaces of wild hills and to drive or 'herd' them precisely where the shepherd wishes them to go.

In ancient times, flocks were in great danger from wolves. They still are in some areas of the continent. So large and powerful dogs were needed, bold and fierce enough to see off a wolf or tackle him if he disputed the challenge.

I often wonder if the 'Shepherd' in German Shepherds does not owe its origin to this. I was born just before the First World War broke out, and I remember our soldiers bringing back Alsatian Wolfhounds as trophies of war. They had been trained and used as superb guard dogs by the German army, who started the Great War with six thousand trained dogs for guarding, taking messages through heavy fire and other unpleasant tasks.

Such guard dogs were naturally fierce, and they got a bad name because, in incompetent hands, they were liable to bite the wrong people. As our wet magistrates have long had the eccentricity of caring more about the welfare of villains than the victims they aimed to rob, the aggressive nature of alsatians fell into disfavour. So alsatians were saddled with the title Alsatian Sheep Dogs, to soften their marketable image.

Those who exhibit their offspring in so-called 'beauty' classes like them called German Shepherds, since the national title German is less offensive now that we are all happy partners of the Common Market instead of antagonists on the battlefield! The fact remains that hip dysplasia became so rife in the breed that whelps are still almost unsaleable without a certificate warranting that they are bred from parents which have been X-rayed and certified free of hip dysplasia. The police told me that they have had to reject as many as forty per cent of dogs offered to them, because of this unacceptable weakness.

Steps taken by the International Sheep Dog Society to eradicate hereditary Progressive Retinal Atrophy were so successful that there is surely only one reason that other hereditary complaints cannot be eradicated in show dogs of other breeds. Money!

Since selective breeding is essentially a matter of compromise, where some faults are tolerated in exchange for exaggerating what a breed standard lays down as 'beauty', those who show dogs for profit would lose out if their dogs, which look pretty but have hidden defects, had selling prices deflated. I prefer the aggressive guard nature of the alsatians of my youth, to the German Shepherds which slink round

*Two camera interview with a competitor after his trial.*

modern show rings, and I hope that the working sheep dogs which earn their living by their deeds in the hills do not suffer the same fate as alsatians which were able and willing to guard their native flocks against wolves and human rustlers.

There are, of course, other types of sheep dogs besides those which were selectively bred to guard the flocks or for the sophisticated manoevres demanded of dogs which can take directions by the remote controls of voice or whistle, hundreds of yards away.

Before the mechanised days of cattle trucks, first by rail and then, motorised, by road, sheep and cattle were fed and fattened sometimes hundreds of miles from centres of population where their carcasses would eventually be consumed.

Reference to old maps will find 'Drovers Roads', running directly to centres of population from remote hills or rich pastures. Beef for the London market was fattened on the lush grazing of the Norfolk marshes and then driven, on foot, to Smithfield, where it was killed.

The old Drovers' Ways often had very wide grass verges each side of the road because the distances to be covered were so great that the stock not only had to feed on the road but they had to be given time to chew their cud and digest it.

118

*Interview over. Cameras concentrate on shots that matter – of the dog!! – for cutaways when interview is edited.*

In 1983 Asa Pinney, a journalist, tried the experiment of driving a bunch of fifty Cheviot sheep the whole way down historic drovers' ways, from Fife, in Scotland, to Exmoor, to discover how sheep and dogs stood up to the journey, which took from March to August. I met him when he got into our neck of the woods, near Burton-on-Trent, in Staffordshire, and he said that, on the traditional drovers' ways, down the Pennines, all had been well, and that the hooves of the sheep appeared to have grown at an abnormal rate to compensate for wear. He still had forty-nine of his original fifty sheep, one having been knocked out by a speeding car. An unusual fate for sheep on a drovers' road!

The dogs' feet had suffered worse than the sheep's, especially on the few miles of newly stoned tarmac after the droveway down the Pennines had petered out into roads designed for motor cars.

Research had shown that stock moved about ten miles in the day at about four miles an hour gave the animals time to feed, chew the cud, and recuperate without losing too much condition on the journey.

Drovers on the flat East Anglian roads, from the Fenlands to Smithfield, passed through wonderful country for hares. The dogs they used were not little Border collie types because their problems were not delicate exercises in finding strays lying up in deep cover and piloting them on intricate routes through boulders, where it was all too easy to put them in a cul-de-sac or push them over the edge of a precipice.

On droveways, the problem was to push on the laggards of large flocks, when brute force could triumph over ignorance and delicate finesse was at a discount. So larger dogs, on the lines of bob-tailed sheep dogs or bearded collies, were in demand and, because stock was allowed long periods to cud and recuperate, drovers and their dogs were only occupied part time on the job on hand.

As a result, the drovers' dogs were crossed with greyhounds to make lurchers of the finest type. They were tough, with enormous stamina and fast enough to catch the hares which proliferated along their drovers' ways. The dogs not only 'lived off the country' on the rabbits and hares they caught, but their masters did not go short either.

These dogs became so famous that their descendants are still often advertised as Smithfield lurchers and, if they are no longer used for droving cattle, they are still beyond compare at catching hares!

When railways got into their stride, it became commercially sound to move sheep and cattle in bulk in cattle trucks on railways, and I should like to conclude this chapter about dogs (and their handlers!) by quoting in full a letter I received from a complete stranger who actually worked as a drover dealing with the Irish cattle trade in Dublin. I quote exactly as he wrote; I also recorded it in my book *It's a Dog's Life*.

> Dear Sir,
> I am writing to you because of your obvious love of working dogs and because I want to record a way of life with dogs which has become extinct.
>
> I was born and reared beside the Dublin cattle market which, in the forties and fifties, was reputed to be the biggest cattle market outside of Chicago.
>
> There were various dogs and types of dogs and different types of drovers, in fact there was a rigid hierarchy existing in the market. First of all you had the Top men. They were retained by the big dealers. They organised the big mobs for the docks and rail and were always addressed as Mister, but only when they were in charge of a mob. They normally only had one dog, generally a blue heeler – this was called a yard dog. This dog only normally worked on a drive

120

when the Top man was in charge of the drive. The rest of the time he worked in the lairs or yard. The Top man would not take charge unless the mob was at least twenty-five animals, and some considered it was beneath their dignity to take charge of less than a hundred head.

Then you had the Button men. These were the regular professional drovers. They were often father and son or brothers. They normally had three heelers between them, one top dog and two flankers. They were essentially freelance but would have a special relationship with one or more Top men and were drovers for generations. Lastly, you had the casuals, generally out of work men, hoping to make a few shillings. There were casual dogs, but they were restricted to moving small groups of cattle to the rail, normally three or four animals. Under any circumstances they would not be allowed on a 'mob'.

The Button men would never have anything to do with sheep or pigs, they would go hungry first. This I suppose is essentially about the Button man and his dogs, so in future, when I refer to man or dog, I am referring to the Button man and his dogs.

The requirements of a good droving dog are different from a sheep dog, as they say you hunt cattle and herd sheep. The dog had to be hard, tough, with tremendous stamina, he had to have great courage and at the same time he had to be absolutely obedient. He had to be big enough and strong enough to put a full grown beast on its back, nine times out of ten the first time (this was done by running a beast and jumping on its neck and knocking it down), but viciousness was not tolerated.

The dog was normally, as far as we were concerned, a cross between a laborador and blue heeler. This gave us the above requirements plus the extra intelligence from the labrador. Some people used only labradors, some blue heelers, some used alsatian cross. However, there was no real prejudice. One of the best dogs we ever had was a little Wicklow collie.

The dog was acquired when it was two years old. We never schooled it as such, it just learned from the other dogs. For the first two or three weeks, we kept it on a rope when we were driving a mob, as an inexperienced dog was dangerous. Of course he got plenty of nourishment from the stick during this period, as he always seemed to be in the way. There never was a conscious time when you said 'Ah, he's ready'. He just evolved naturally and, as I said, learned from the other dogs. Due to the harshness of the work, most dogs were put down before their sixth year. This was due to long hours, wet, wind and continuous work. As soon as the dog showed wakeness (weakness) he was put down. Of course he stood a good chance of being crippled or maimed before that. But no man took any pleasure in putting down a good servant – and the better the servant, the sooner he cracked up. It was a kindness to put them down. The local vet charged two shillings to put a dog down but five shillings to put one down while you held him, with an injection. Even though five shillings was a lot of money, I never heard of a dog being put down for two shillings.

*The Working Week*
From midday Monday, groups of cattle would start arriving by rail and by road for the market to be held on Wednesday. We would work one dog at a time to get the cattle to the holding lairs or auction lairs. We rotated the dogs often so as not to wear them out. That evening we gave them a feed, feeding each dog separately.

*Tuesday*, the pressure of work built up as cattle arrived from all over Ireland. From ten in the morning it would be non-stop. We still, if possible, used only one dog, rotating. Invariably we ended up using two dogs or, as we used to say, one-and-a-half dogs, with shorter rest and work periods. That finished about midnight. Each dog got a pint of boiled milk with whisky in it.

*Wednesday 3.30 am.* As they say in Gaelic, 'Do rogai se mar so' – 'this is what they were born for'. Bring cattle from lairs to auction yards, cattle from outlying holding fields to market. The chaos of the market as mob met mob and dogs struggled to keep them separate, non stop, hour after hour, as cattle were moved, and moved again, the dogs worked. By this time the market would be a river of liquid manure and the dogs would be covered and every chance they got to lay down and rest, their great lolling tongues hanging half a yard out of the side of their mouths and that happy, smiling look that only hard worked dogs seem to have.

About 11.30 things began to calm down and there would be time for a pint, half of Guinness for the dogs in summer and rum and warm water in winter. Then back to the fray. Then it was the reverse of procedures, as cattle went to rail and back to lairs and outlying fields, slaughterhouses, anywhere. Deep in the market, three or four big mobs were being marshalled, each top man controlling and counting his mob as cattle were brought by the button men from auction yards around the market. These were the mobs for the docks and England and they were to be driven, when they were all assembled, through the centre of Dublin city.

Depending on how good a market it was, there would be between three hundred and five hundred head in each mob. If the market was good, there would not be enough button men for each mob, and the top men would decide which mob would go first. On a drive, each man only used one dog, the top dog. The others were left at home because you couldn't hold tight on three dogs with this size of mob. So you would have five button men and their dogs, the top man and his heeler, and half a dozen casuals. We moved off, the pointsman and his dog leading, he set the pace at a very fast walk, the cattle following with their noses nearly touching the dog's tail.

A good point dog was, as you can imagine, hard to come by. The trick was to form a perfect spearhead shape. This was done by the front flankers, a man and dog, at each side, near the front. The rear flankers' job was to patrol the flank and prevent a breakaway from the mob. If a beast did break away it was most important that the dog did not get between the beast and the mob. The top man pushed from the rear and was in command; by easing back a little, he lengthened the spearhead, and by pushing he shortened it. Two casuals pushed with the top man and the four other casuals' main task was to block side roads and gateways.

That's the theory of it, however the reality was a nightmare. If you can imagine five hundred head of cattle being driven through the West End of London, in the rush hour, you would have some idea of the problem. The biggest single hazard was parked cars. Imagine a beast breaking and getting isolated from the mob, by parked cars, and a woman with a pram on the pavement. Now add a dog, pushing the beast, and you have the makings of a drover's nightmare. That's why such close order was taken on each dog. We had only one command, 'Behind,' and woe betide any dog that did not obey instantly. Unlike sheep dogs, we had no complicated orders. We never whistled. We cursed, we shouted, we had conversations, but only one command, 'Behind'.

Let's face it, when you work a dog in eighteen hour stretches and for five or six days a week, and you are with them every working minute, you don't need any orders, they know what you're thinking even when you're not there. I can recall some amazing stories about them. However, we've not finished in the market. When the docks were reached, the animals were penned. This again was hard, dangerous work, as the animals did not like being separated.

What I forgot to tell you was that every button man and top man on a dock drive pushed an old battered lady's bike, without a crossbar. This could be mounted in a hurry to run down a beast, and at the same time provided transport back from the docks. The funny thing was to see a group of drovers returning from the docks on their bikes, the dogs trotting behind, three-quarter ways on, they didn't trot

123

straight, but partly sideways. Their tongues hanging down the side, and all the dogs fast asleep on their feet. Back home, leave the top dogs and pick up the others, and back to the market for the bits and pieces, the cleaning up.

Then home, to pick up all the dogs and into the pub. The paying out was done from the pub, and I won't bore you with the ramifications of the financial set-up, sufficient to say that they make the financial details of the City look like a housewife's budget. Each dog got either a large rum and water or a pint of Guinness. Each set of drovers had their own pub, and each pub had a dog room.

The dogs retired to the dog room to sleep. Picture a pig sty, with twenty pigs lying over, under and on top of each other. Well, convert the pigs to manure-covered dogs, and you have the picture, and steam rising off them, as if they were being boiled. No food.

*Thursday.* No food, by this time the dogs would be gaunt, but there was always some work on Thursday morning, but steady work, without pressure. Back home at lunch time, the dogs still caked with manure, were hosed down and examined for ticks, cuts etc. The big copper that had been boiled all morning was tipped into a trough, maby thirty to fifty pounds of meat and offal, and the dogs ate. They were trencher-fed, and did they eat. Within half an hour they would be gorged. They would sometimes be so bloated that they would not be able to move to their bed.

*Friday* was a fast day, no food at all, and by evening they would be just coming round.

*Saturday,* each dog fed separately and checked to see how much weight he had lost, and given extra food if he needed it. There was always some work on Saturday, never enough to extend a dog, but we'd always use the fittest one.

*Sunday* was a day of rest for the dogs. Plenty of grub. Some exercise but gentle exercise, a walk rather than a run. That was an average week.

As I said at the beginning, it's a lifestyle that has vanished, mainly due to the cattle transporter. I'm not sorry it's gone, it was a hard, brutal life for man and beast. However, I mark the passing of these great-hearted dogs with this letter because they were good servants and willing slaves.

Mr Drabble, I'm sure you understand that I'm not a writing man and this letter is written in kindness for the dogs, so I hope you will read it with the same kindness and ignore the spelling etc.

One last thing, if you ever have occasion to refer to anything in this letter, please don't mention my name, as writing a letter like this would be considered a mark of weakness among my peers in Dublin and would cause me embarrassment.

*Yours faithfully,*

Respecting his wishes, I leave his name anonymous, but I feel that his account paints a picture of dogs which became extinct because of mechanisation. An entirely different type of herding dog to the collies we see so often on the screen, etched as vividly as by any television camera.

My own Rottweiler, as tough and hard-bitten a dog as any I have known, comes from a line of similar drovers' dogs, used for generations on the continent, where cattle were driven for great distances to the city of Rottweil, which was the centre of the cattle trade.

They were bred from strains of dogs used for boar hunting, which was a sport where brawn triumphed over brain and courage was paramount.

The story goes that, when the drovers were paid off, their prime desire was to celebrate by having a monumental booze-up, ending stoned out of their minds, and theoretically prime targets for thugs or pickpockets to relieve them of their earnings.

They defeated such risks by the highly practical ruse of keeping only what cash they intended to spend on celebration. The rest was rolled into a tight packet and pouched in a container built into their dog's collar. Anyone who could steal the master's money from the dog's collar more than earned his loot.

So the drovers' dogs of Dublin and Rottweil, the poaching sheep dogs known as Smithfields, or Norfolk Lurchers from East Anglia, old English bulldogs which could not only 'throw' a beast but pin him, immobile, by the nose, dogs such as alsatians, bred to guard the flocks against wolves and rustlers, and our beloved border collies, were all 'sheep' or 'cattle' dogs, as different from each other as chalk from cheese, because each had a totally different task to perform.

I find the idea of downgrading a sensitive, highly intelligent collie to herding cattle, when he is past being an equal partner in the sophisticated world of sheep dog trialling, very upsetting. A sideways swipe from a cow's hind foot could break a leg or put an eye out, while dealing with a protective suckler cow, determined her calf shall be kept sacrosanct. That is work for canine thugs, not artists in their field.

# 5
# Country Connections

THE WIDESPREAD hunger for anything wholesome and traditional, with deep enough roots to be an anchor, is often highlighted by viewers' reaction to evidence of craftsmanship.

One magazine item in almost every series deals with shepherds' crooks, and the volume of letters it unfailingly produces is a yardstick of the admiration which is felt for such works of art, which combine elegance with excellence of work.

Crooks are tools of the shepherd's trade which, like scythes or woodmen's axes, are so functional and so simple that the cleverest modern boffin has never been able to better them. They are beautiful to look at, satisfying to touch, and in no way inferior to the finest works of art.

Whether shepherds led their flocks, as in biblical days, or drove them, as today, a crook was vital to capture a sheep at close quarters, when a minute examination was vital. The biblical connection still continues in the form of a bishop's crozier, which is the symbol of his care and responsibility for his human flock.

It is not surprising, therefore, that shepherds are so devoted to their profession and so proud of their competitive expertise that, when work is done, there is no relaxation they enjoy better than proving to their fellows (and the world!) that their dogs and their skills reign supreme.

Such exhibitions, like major sheep dog trials, are not conducted in sloppy dress. The modern fashionable trendies, on such occasions, turn up in 'casual' attire, often in blue denims of cloth inferior in quality to overalls worn by garage mechanics.

The tails of their open-necked multi-coloured shirts flap forlornly outside their trousers, and their feet are clad in sloppy 'trainers',

126

though for what they are in training is obscure. To make themselves even more conspicuous, they sport gaudy anoraks, designed for easy identification by mountain rescue squads.

Regulars at formal rural shows or trials are smartly but not expensively turned out when they appear in public. Jacket and collar and tie are well pressed, however ancient. Caps and functional all-weather clothes spell out the fact that neither their work nor their leisure are dependent on what the weatherman forecasts.

Their shepherds' crooks have staffs, or 'shanks' of ash or hazel of precisely the right length for their particular function. What is 'right' for a man who walks tens of miles a day, in rugged hill country, would not be right for use on level lowlands or for leaning on at market. Each must be the comfortable, functional length to suit the individual, who may be tall, angular and athletic, or short, cloddy and getting on in years.

This is easy enough to achieve by starting off with a shank that is definitely too long, so that it can be nibbled shorter, half an inch at a time, until the owner feels that it is perfectly comfortable and fashioned to fit his needs with the care and skill of a Savile Row tailor.

But a crook is not simply a delightful 'third leg' to ease the passage of its owner over terrain of infinite variety. It is a tool of the shepherd's trade, specifically designed for catching sheep, stopping them in full flight if necessary.

The aesthetically curving crook head is designed for this purpose, perfection having been evolved through centuries of trial and error.

There should be room to pass a man's four fingers between the nose of the horn head and the neck, where it joins the wooden shank, and the curve inside should take the back of a man's hand. These dimensions will obviously vary for the breed of sheep the shepherd handles, because a large enough gap to pass over the neck of a great lowland breed and hold the captive immobile, would be big enough to allow active little hill sheep to wriggle free in seconds. Crooks for individual shepherds, of varying shapes and sizes, and for different stamps of sheep, are chosen with the skill of racehorse owners and trainers selecting horses for courses.

Although the general shapes of the heads will be similar and the shanks will be tailored for their owners, the relative size of head and shank will be fashioned so that the combined balance is perfect, because the task of catching a heavy, bolting ewe, swerving at full gallop, will be next to impossible with a ill-balanced, top-heavy, clumsy

*The crook presented to me, and fashioned by Fred Prickett who loves the programme.*

crook, but will be a source of great pride with a tool so 'right' that it inspires dexterity.

To make such a tool requires the craftsmanship of a cabinet maker and the expertise of a plastic surgeon.

Sheep horns, which are the basic material of the finest crook handles, come in all sorts of sizes and conditions. The horns of hoary old rams are the best, the older the better, provided they were healthy and without injury when they died. Sadly, when an old ram's useful life is over, his carcase still fetches good money, and he is culled far younger than were rams a generation ago, which were worth no more than a drink for carting them to the nearest foxhound kennels.

Scottish Blackface and Swaledale have spiralling horns which make superb basic raw material but need skill and imagination in reshaping for utility and form. Jacob sheep have less bone but give scope for originality of design, which still retains its fitness of purpose. Goat horns and buffalo, and the diminishing number of breeds of cattle still left to mature as nature intended, can all produce satisfactory raw material, but the end product still depends upon skill as much as on imagination.

Hazel or ash or blackthorn or holly sticks do not all grow as straight as the shanks of traditional shepherds' crooks. So stick-makers seem to have a third eye which concentrates on nothing but its ceaseless search for potential walking sticks and crook shanks, whatever may be the official business in hand. Taking a stick, like picking a panful of mushrooms, is not classed as stealing, in the country, and the time to take a stick is when you see it. Those who leave good sticks to improve with age are liable to find them gone when they return to harvest them!

Ideally, they should be picked in late autumn and winter when the sap is down – and then be left a year to dry out, if necessary suspended, tied in bundles of ten or twelve, or individually, head uppermost, with a weight suspended from the lower end, to 'stretch' it straight while it is seasoning.

The final straightening of the shank, or bending the head into a crook shape for wooden crooks with no horn handle, is accomplished by heating, till soft, and bending over a jig of the desired shape, and leaving to cool while so constrained.

Horn can also be shaped while softened by heat, steam or flame being traditional for horn, though a box of hot, moist sand is sometimes used on wood.

129

The makers of some of the finest bone-headed crooks often use methylated spirit flame to mould the rough shape they want, raising the temperature locally until the horn is too hot to hold firmly, in bare hands, but so that they can still bear to touch it. A whole collection of shaped jigs and vices and metal clamps are used for the basic discipline of shape, but the details are produced with metal rasps and files and razor-sharp blades.

Visualise the old time craftsmen, before television had been invented to waste time on endless soaps on the box, with political pundits prattling doom and gloom. The only illumination in isolated cottages would have been the soft light of an oil lamp, which would also have supplied manipulative heat if the bone was held close over the top of the lamp glass. What better way was there of whiling away long winter evenings than by whittling the uncouth blemishes of venerable rams' horns until manual skill converted them into perfect crooks to discipline the descendents of the rams which grew the horns.

It was but a short step to turn such purely functional crooks into minor masterpieces. The general shape of a crook handle needs little imagination to turn it into a leaping trout or pheasant's head.

Among the pleasantest surprises I ever had was when I was approached in a pub at Grisedale, in the Lake District, by a perfect stranger who introduced himself as Fred Prickett. 'I heard you were coming,' he said, 'and, as I've enjoyed the sheep dog programmes so much, I thought I'd make you this.'

'This' turned out to be a superb shepherd's crook with a rich hazel shank and ram's horn handle which had been beautifully carved. A seated dog had been carved from the solid horn at the nose of the crook, and he was watching three sheep, carved on top of the crown. They were being driven towards a pen, which was carved just above where the crook had been dowelled into the shank.

Crooks with figures carved from the solid with great delicacy, can take two or three hundred hours of limitless patience, so that such a gift from a stranger was a great compliment to everyone connected with the programme, from the competitors – and their dogs! – before the camera to backroom boys behind the scenes. It is among my most treasured possessions.

Some of the crooks which win prizes in competitions are even more intricate. Norman Tulip, among the very top flight in his craft of 'stick dressing', does plain(!) crooks of the utmost delicacy, with perhaps a single thistle on the nose and the owner's name carved upon the crown. Such 'plain' sticks rely for their attraction on their perfect symmetry and balance and the way the horn head blends into the shank as if they had grown together. He does the conventional pheasants' heads and writhing trout, but he also does birds of miraculous delicacy, worthy of Grinling Gibbons. One stick that he fashioned has two horses and carts, carved from the solid, with a waggoner in charge of the first horse. Another was a traditional hoop-shaped gypsy caravan with two horses, a pony, a lurcher and a gypsy woman on the nose, where the thistle often is.

Norman Tulip's appetite for such work is insatiable. A stick with a most beautiful lobster on the heel and a fish on the nose being particularly intricate.

When we show such sophisticated rural art in the programme, it is not surprising that we are absolutely inundated with letters from viewers wanting the address of the dresser who can produce such sticks, asking to buy one or learn to make one for themselves.

They are often disappointed, because although such craftsmen love nothing better than stick dressing, there is no abomination worse to them than replying to letters from strangers. So it is the policy of the BBC to forward correspondence with no guarantee that it will be answered, and nothing will induce them to divulge where such artists live. My publishers have the same policy.

Despite such discouragement, the popularity of stick dressing has grown so rapidly that those interested have formed the British Stickmakers' Guild, Greenacre, Station Road, Beaconsfield, Bucks. HP9 1LG. This has been formed to exchange information, produce a newsletter and give sources of supply of specialist materials. If you wish for further information, please write to them not me!

Although such conventional crooks, skilfully used, are ideal for catching sheep in the open, the leg-cleek is extremely handy for picking a particular sheep from a bunch at close quarters.

The 'cleek', or crook, is only just wide enough in the mouth to go round a proper old penny piece, from the days before our currency was converted to worthless decimal washers, to suit foreigners the other side of the Channel. This may seem pretty small to go round a sheep's leg, but it was found just right to slip over the narrow part of the hind leg, just above the knee, so that the animal could be gently yanked backwards out of the bunch. If the mouth was too big, it allowed the animal to struggle and twist, in imminent peril of breaking a leg.

Such leg cleeks were too small for satisfactory ornamentation, and small enough to make the task of dowelling the crook to the shank rather difficult. So many leg cleeks were purely working tools, fashioned by the blacksmith, but none the worse for that. The fitness for their purpose was so precise and economical of effort that they are things of beauty in the same sense as scythes and axes and other instruments of country craftsmen's trade.

The popularity of demonstrations of stick dressing encouraged Ian Smith to include other aspects of sheep husbandry in the programme, so that we have visited Gordon Beningfield on several occasions.

Gordon is an old personal friend of mine and a distinguished artist who is particularly fond of the Hardy Country, immortalised in Hardy's Wessex novels about rural life in Tess of the d'Urberville's days.

Like many of our viewers, including me, Gordon is fascinated by everything to do with shepherding, which is surely one of the most traditional forms of stockmanship which has been less diluted by science than almost any other branch. The obscenities of feeding sheep on hormones to produce more milk or to accelerate growth of heavier tasteless carcases are thankfully scientific horrors of the future.

Gordon puts more of his money where his mouth is than most of us are prepared to do, perhaps because such born artists thrive on visual images. He has no chi-chi summerhouse to impress the neighbours, but a slightly decrepit shed instead, which turns out to be far more exclusive. The shed at the bottom of Gordon's garden does not look out of place, because it is surrounded not by serried rows of spuds or formal bedding-out plants, but by butterflies instead, attracted there by the profusion of wild flowers, native to the English countryside.

They are the same wild flowers – or their descendents – as those that graced the shed when it started life, generations of countrymen ago, as a shepherd's hut on wheels, designed to be dragged out into the fields by carthorses, so that a shepherd, its original occupant, could literally live among his sheep, for weeks on end, while they were lambing. Just the sort of hut that could have belonged to Gabriel Oaks on Hardy's Norcombe Hill, which appears on the map as Toller Down.

Ian conceived the idea of Gordon and I sitting in the shepherd's hut at the bottom of his garden, discussing the shepherding memorabilia he has collected during the years he has been fascinated by anything to do with sheep and shepherding.

The idea worked admirably because, sitting in that cramped little hut, looking at old branding irons for sheep, hoof trimmers and cook

132

pots heated by the little cast iron stove, we soon forgot the camera was spying on us and the microphone eavesdropping. As Gordon showed me the horn lanterns used long before electric torches – or even paraffin lamps – we shared his discoveries and our mutual love of rural bye-gones with uncounted viewers in their homes.

My good fortune was that the visit was so well received that it has been repeated by popular request and, each time I go, both the viewers and I get a little closer to the deep countryside by looking at it through Gordon's artist's eyes.

The sort of thing which delights his eyes is a superb little oak costrel, which was a perfect miniature oak barrel. It was not in his shepherd's hut but had a place of honour on the sideboard in the house. Each stave of the barrel was perfectly curved and shaved to butt with its neighbour, to be as leakproof as a brewer's barrel fashioned by a cooper. When the staves were shaved to fit, they were held immovably in place by steel hoops, as normal barrels are, and because the craftsmanship was superb and the proportions so good, it was as much a thing of beauty as any fine piece of antique furniture.

Its function was prosaic, for it was made to hold about a quart of cider, which could be drunk straight from the costrel through a little wooden spout. The shepherds who Gordon so much admired took provisions for the day when they went out to work, cider in their costrels and food in enamel basins, carried as a rule in a red handkerchief with white spots.

Not everything in the countryside, of course, is pleasant, nor ever has been. Sound stockmanship does not only entail birth, at lambing time, and the skill and devotion to rear stock under good conditions of health and hygiene. It entails death as well, when the crop is ready for fattening and ripe for the butcher.

So one year, we went to the sheep sale at Dolgellau in North Wales, to see hundreds of lambs brought down from wild hills to be put under the auctioneer's hammer. This is the sheep farmer's harvest as much as corn is on arable farms.

However practical and unimaginative a stockman may be, it is natural to feel twinges of regret when a crop of lambs, on which he has spent countless sleepless nights and uncomfortable rainy days, are going to the slaughterhouse. But the hyped-up urgency of the auctioneer, intoning rising bids, and the shouting bustle of the market, drown out such sentiment, so that satisfaction with success obliterates depression.

But for me the scene turned sour. As pens of lambs were knocked down to the highest bidder, a man arrived, armed with a tool like saddlers use to punch round holes in leather. That, it appears, was his specific purpose; his function in life was to punch round holes, about as large as a fingernail, not in dead, unfeeling leather, but through live lambs' ears. There was nothing to deaden the pain. One second the lamb was at worst scared by its strange surroundings. The next second it was shaking its head, spattering its fellows with blood from the hole punched without warning through its ear. Fleshy platelets which had completed the lobes were lying in the mud like plastic discs discarded after children's games of tiddlywinks.

Nobody – but the lambs and I – appeared to notice. When I enquired what lay behind such barbarity, I was told that it was the Ministry's safeguard against paying subsidy on the same lamb twice.

The old country custom of diddling authority had apparently been adapted so that a batch of lambs could be sent to market one week, sold to a fictitious butcher to collect some stupid Common Market subsidy, after which they were taken home again, so that the swindle could be repeated next week. Although the lambs were put to the inconvenience of a weekly trip to market, at least they did not have their throats slit and their owner was reimbursed for his enterprise when he was presented with several government subsidies on the same batch of lambs. Bureaucracy eventually tumbled to the fact that they were being fleeced by the sheep farmers, so some Smart Alec, in his feather-bedded office, pointed out how easy it would be to plug the financial leak. 'Put a hole in their ear,' he said, 'the first time subsidy is paid, and refuse payment for any lamb which already has a hole in either ear'.

The chap who was performing the operation looked unimaginative, to put it kindly. But the real villain, in my eyes, was the faceless little bumblecrat who had sentenced countless innocent lambs to such cold-blooded mutilation to save a few pieces of silver being filched from authority by petty thieves intent on fiddling the books. I should love to have forced the bureaucrat concerned to see what misery his 'efficiency' caused until, spattered with blood, he crawled away to think of something better, and I would cheerfully have punched a hole in his ear to concentrate his mind.

The wide boys drawing multiple subsidies must have been in a minority which would shrink to nothing if a few were caught and slapped in gaol to cool their heels. And it would not need the mind of

134

a genius to produce an indelible dye or tattoo to register which animals had been subsidised, without any need for operations performed without so much as a local anaesthetic.

Leaning on the market railings was a lady who took no part in the bidding, seemed to have no lambs herself, and who was quite obviously above such petty pilfering. We struck up a conversation, and I discovered she was a shepherdess, out on a busman's holiday, not to work her dog in competition or to compete in classes for the most proficient stick-dresser. This was not the place for either. She was a visitor, like me, whose idea of a holiday was to go to a sheep sale, remote from the Leicestershire farm where she was employed, to see how sheep prices compared with those in the markets which she normally used.

Like so many livestock farmers, her heart was so much in her work that there was nothing she would rather do. I took her address and made a date to meet her in the spring.

She is Sheilah Ellis and her employer runs a flock of five hundred and twenty ewes on his farm near Oakham, which bureaucrats class as Leicestershire but civilised local inhabitants still regard as Rutland.

The ewes do not lamb out in the field but are brought into a covered yard divided into small hurdle enclosures, as was the auction yard in Wales when we met.

By anybody's standards, five hundred and twenty sheep is a large flock to manage at lambing time, and plenty of shepherds would want assistants who could work in shifts, right round the clock. Sheilah Ellis is made of sterner stuff. When we called to see her, near the end of the lambing season, she had lambed five hundred ewes and got nine hundred and ninety seven live lambs. She was hoping for three sets of triplets amongst the last twenty ewes, which would knock the flock average up to two lambs a ewe, which is very high indeed.

Some yardstick for comparison is that plenty of hill sheep, left to lamb on their own, as their ancestors did, have a job to rear a lamb a ewe, and many lowland farmers would not turn up their noses at one and a half lambs average.

Nor did Sheilah fritter away potential profits by feather-bedding herself with surplus labour. She managed with one youth who was gaining practical experience while at agricultural college.

When we called, she hadn't been to bed for more than three weeks! She was out in the lamb yard from 6am to 6pm, taking thermos and sandwiches as sustenance. Then she went home to her cottage, half a mile or so from the sheep yard, leaving the youth to keep the flag flying.

She cooked herself a meal and settled down in a chair by the fire for a doze, her sheep dog curled in comfort on the rug. She had a bottle of scotch by her side. At eleven she went back to the yard to sort out any problems beyond the scope of her assistant, who took his turn to rest. When everything was running smoothly, she returned to her comforts by the fire and cat-napped the night away – except for doing her rounds at 1 and 3am! At six, she was back on full-time duty.

When each ewe showed signs of lambing, it was separated from the flock and put into a small pen – which Sheilah called her maternity ward – to get individual supervision while lambing and passing the 'cleansings' or afterbirth.

Ewes which had only a single lamb were fastened by the head, as cows were tethered in old-fashioned cowsheds for milking. This was to prevent them turning round and butting the strange lamb which their shepherdess removed, as surplus, from a more ambitious ewe which had obliged by producing three. Rearing three lambs is a great strain on the ewe, so it is customary to take the surplus (some have four and, exceptionally, five!) and foster them onto ewes which only have one – or none, if the sole lamb dies.

Ewes left loose would not accept the foster lambs unless their own dead lamb is skinned and the skin fitted, as an overcoat, to fool the ewe by smelling like her own.

But, if they are tethered as soon as their single lamb is on his feet, clever shepherds – or shepherdesses, like Sheilah – can foster a surplus lamb onto them. When it has suckled, and her milk passed through it, it acquires her odour, and her yoke can be removed because she will no longer be able to tell she has been conned into fostering a changeling.

When the lambs are a few days old, and strong on their feet, the ewes and lambs are removed from their maternity pens and taken to fresh grass paddocks near the yard. In good weather they will be fine, but the lambs' wool has not yet acquired its waterproof lanoliney texture; they are still too small to retain much body heat, so that, in cold wet weather, they become sodden and are in grave danger of death from hypothermia.

---

*A ewe restrained by a yoke to prevent her butting her foster lamb till her milk has passed through it and has acquired her maternal scent. The lamb peeps through the slot in the yoke.*

Once more Sheilah comes to the rescue. In the calms between the bouts of parturition, she cuts out little 'lamb coats' from the plastic bags which contained artificial fertilisers for the arable fields on the farm. Before they are turned out from the sheep yard, the lambs are fitted with their plastic coats, looking, for all the world, like miniature racehorses, turned out to grass in brightly coloured horse rugs. Such touches of finesse spell the difference between an average of two lambs reared per ewe and a less spectacular or profitable one and a half! As in so many other spheres, the difference between profit and loss has as much to do with perspiration as more spectacular inspiration.

Such insights into the less glamorous periods of a shepherd's life do much to heighten the appreciation of feats on the trials field, and we found that viewers were simply enthralled by Sheilah's skill and dedication to her flock. Nor were we alone in our esteem, because in 1987 she was included in the honoured guest list of those invited to attend the luncheon for Woman of the Year, and, having seen her work first hand, I can vouch for the fact that it was indeed a compliment well earned.

Working with such pleasant countryfolk, in such attractive places, makes it seem invidious for me to recount particular relish derived from some without mentioning them all, but I have just chosen a few at random.

Among my most pleasant expeditions was with Ian Smith and Gordon Beningfield, to visit Ken Beckingham, a friend of Gordon's, who had a marvellous collection of sheep bells, which reminded me of my childhood days on the Wiltshire downs above the White Horse of Bratton, near Westbury.

We often stayed with my uncle, who was a doctor at Bratton, at the foot of the downs, which were then mile after rolling mile of close-cropped turf, studded with a profusion of wild flowers, which loved the chalky soil. Defilement by poisonous chemicals, which obliterated wildlife and could not distinguish between pestilential weeds and harmless native wild flowers, was still a vandal boffin's dream. So was the ploughing up of the ancient natural grassland to grow corn to make corn mountains even higher.

At the bottom end of August or early September, thousands of sheep, on the hoof, converged near the chalk White Horse, for the annual Westbury Sheep Fair. There were no cattle trucks, in those days, so men and dogs drove the sheep there – and we used to hear them coming long before they arrived, because a few animals in each flock

138

were fitted with a leather collar which had been rivetted to a sheep bell.

It was impossible for the sheep to move without jangling the bell and, as no two bells had the same note, every shepherd knew the sound as well as the sight of his own individual sheep.

They were simple steel bells, made by the local blacksmith for a few pence, and the custom was for them to be owned by the shepherd and not his master.

Agricultural labourers were hired at special annual 'hiring' fairs, and the contract of service covered a year and was sealed by a handshake and a shilling, given by the master to his new man. There was no such thing as gazumping in those days, and a bargain, once struck, was binding for a year, when either party might decide a change was indicated. The sound of sheep bells carried for miles over the downs, in the still evening air, and we used to wander up at dusk before the fair, to watch the sheep being penned in wattle hurdles, ready to be sold.

The downs were not fenced, so, for the rest of the year, the local shepherds brought their flocks to graze sward owned or rented by their master, before and after the annual Westbury sheep fair.

The leaders of these sheep wore bells, and we used to listen to them as the shepherds and their dogs moved the flock out onto open downland soon after dawn, and brought them back near the farmstead when dusk approached.

The beauty of such bells was that each had its own distinctive pitch and note, and so that the shepherd could locate the sheep that was wearing it, even if she was out of sight in a hollow or over the brow of the down. Their utility was that the bells made different sounds, dependent on what the sheep were doing at the time, and the shepherd could 'read' their movements as easily as we could put words to a familiar tune.

The melody bore eloquent testimony that informed the observant shepherd if his flock was lying down, chewing their cud contentedly, or whether they were still moving gently across the sward, feeding as they wended their rhythmic way.

Should disaster strike, of course, and raiding dogs panicked the flock, the random jangling of the bells was as plain in its meaning to the shepherd as a 999 call for help would be to our generation.

I never heard a sheep bell since those childhood downland days until we went to see Ken Beckingham, whose hobby is collecting them.

139

This is not as easy as it might sound, because bells which were made by the local blacksmith for sixpence, ninepence, or a shilling, were often chucked on the scrap heap when the flock was fenced in and there was no further use for them.

But the collection we had come to see seemed to be of infinite variety. There were bells as big as teapots and as small as eggcups.

The small, spherical bells, called rumblers, soon went out of fashion, because their music did not carry far when all was well. In wet weather they soon got baulmed with mud, which muffled them, so that they could not be heard at all.

Cup bells, open at the bottom, but usually cast in brass or bell metal, were considered too effete for sheep, so that the popular bells, which still echo in my memory, were clucklets and canisters, made by the local blacksmith in sheet steel for a palmful of coppers apiece.

When he bent and assembled them, the note could be adjusted by removing metal or by adding brass until they reproduced the precise note the shepherd wanted. The harness to attach the bell to the sheep was fashioned from leather straps – usually 'borrowed' from the stable when the carter had gone home from work.

The shepherd knew the sound of every bell and, for him as well as in my memory, the moving flock composed the melody, which had a wonderfully continuous rhythm but never played the same tune twice. It was the Music of the Downs.

Ken Beckingham's collection was not confined to steel sheep bells but included far more musical horse bells, of cast bell metal. These had played background music to colourful May Day roistering, when children danced round the maypole, horses were done up with ribbons and brasses and bells, and village youths and maidens celebrated as their ancestors and descendants have always revelled in spring.

One particular bell especially took my fancy, because it explained the origin of an ancient rural word which I had never understood – 'Bell Wether'.

A wether sheep corresponds to a gelding horse or a bullock of the bovine species. None of them will ever celebrate the rites of spring again because they have been deprived of the means of doing so. They have all been castrated. The castration of stock is for one, or both, of two reasons. It is usually to tame aggressive instincts, to make the animal safer with men and less aggressive with its own kind. As everybody knows, entire bulls are dangerous and treacherous. 'Milk' breeds like Friesian and dainty Jerseys are worse than 'beef' breeds

*The venerable mobile generator – a valuable part of the equipment.*

like Herefords – but all are too dangerous to take chances with, and people are killed by bulls in the countryside every year.

Apart from the danger to stockmen and visitors, bulls will fight and maim each other if several are left together with the females of their species.

Once deprived of their means of reproduction, their whole nature changes. Bullocks can be safely run together, when they have been castrated, and they are normally as docile as old cows in the presence of people. More docile, in fact, for suckler cows with calves at foot are better avoided than trifled with.

Stallions do not advertise their aggression with threatening horns, but they are at least as dangerous as entire bulls, though fewer people realise it because their beauty masks their menace. The ram, as the inspiration for the term 'battering ram', to denote something which can pulverise all in its path by brute force, is an apt allegory. The clash of skulls when two rams charge each other can be heard half a mile across a valley and, left to themselves, it is not uncommon for one to break his rival's neck.

Since rams cannot be left to run with the flock except at tupping time, male lambs are castrated if there are not plans to use them for stud. They also fatten faster.

It sometimes so happens that one of these lambs is an orphan which has to be reared by hand, as a 'cade' lamb, on the bottle, in which case it will grow up delightfully tame and friendly. It was not uncommon for shepherds to make a favourite pet of such a lamb and keep it for years after its siblings had long since graced the butcher's slab.

These old wethers were incorrigibly greedy, and came from afar whenever they saw the shepherd, expecting a crust or a few sheep nuts from his pocket. Resourceful countrymen also made them earn their keep as eunuch music masters of the flock.

Because an old wether is such a large and powerful brute, it caused him no great inconvenience if a large, distinctive sheep bell was hung around his neck. That is the origin of the term 'Bell Wether', and the shepherd could listen for the familiar chimes and know, by the melody, where the flock was and what it was doing.

It had advantages for other sheep as well. Being no fools, the rest of the flock soon cottoned-on to the fact that, when the shepherd approached, the bell wether sidled up to him with purpose in his stride. He knew that the man who had bottle-reared him still had a soft spot which impelled him to bring some tit-bits, so that any old ewe, joining the party, might glean a few crumbs which fell from the bell wether's table!

This was a great advantage to the shepherd who had taken the trouble to 'cade' and keep a bell wether, because instead of having to round up his flock, if the shepherd rattled a bucket of food, the bell wether would follow him, and the rest of the sheep would follow the bell wether, knowing that where he was there would also be crumbs of goodies from the bucket.

What fun it would be to organise a Bell Wether Stakes where, instead of directing his dog to guide sheep from obstacle to obstacle, the shepherd bribed his bell wether with tasty tit-bits so that the rest of the sheep would follow him round the course. We could call it the Ring Leader Stakes!

It is really quite extraordinary how the wool trade has changed over the centuries. Because we live in an era of ridiculous Common Market subsidies, profit and loss are controlled by political expediency instead of by supply and demand or competitive efficiency.

Until recently, economics dictated that wool and mutton were best produced mainly in hill country, where rocks were too near the surface to plough, and gradients and altitude made conventional agriculture impracticable. So much more profit could be earned from corn on fertile soil, that sheep were pastured on marginal land which would have deteriorated without them.

When politicians poked their noses in so that even incompetents could not go wrong, Jags and Range Rovers became the rural norm, but when surplus mountains grew so high, even the Ministry of Agriculture had to do something about them. The pendulum then swung, and sheep appeared in strength even in our part of the Midlands, which is really rich dairying country of the highest order.

It reminded me of medieval times, when rich merchants in the Cotswolds made vast fortunes off the backs of peasants and sheep. Several Cotswold towns are still monuments to the rich prosperity wool brought. Ian agreed that a portrait of such a place, to illustrate the point, might dovetail with the programme.

We chose Fairford, which is still a thriving market town of about two thousand souls, fashioned from mellow Cotswold stone, though it now makes much of its living from the tourist trade. The modern jargon for such a change is Farm Diversification, though Fairford was practising what we preach long before our politicians latched onto the phrase. The imposing church which is the fulcrum of the town was obviously far too big to be necessary for a scattered agricultural community. That is common enough for such churches, which owe their origin to rich benefactors, who made a fortune large enough to buy public recognition.

There is still an ancient watermill in Fairford, which was built as a wool mill to deal with the woollen harvest which dominated the countryside around. Sitting on the bridge over the stream which fed the mill, I looked across at the town and the huge church which towered above it. John Thame, the man who built the church, was no simple shepherd or farmer. He had a finger in many pies and would doubtless have been a tycoon if he had lived in our own entrepreneurial age.

He had ships to sail his wool to the continent – and sailors who do not seem to have been above a bit of piracy! Apparently, they 'found' a cargo of superb glass which another ship was taking for the Pope, in Rome, and brought it back for their boss in Fairford. Perhaps it was the medieval equivalent of modern goods which are sometimes said to have 'fallen off the back of a lorry'! He was so pleased with the glass that he decided to have it made into stained glass windows and to erect them in the church as a symbol of his success, but there was a minor snag. The church, at that time, was not big enough to house such windows adequately. Nothing daunted Thame, and he pulled down the church and built a new one of generous enough proportions to house his windows superbly. Status symbols are as old as Time.

This magnificent ecclesiastical showcase for the cargo of stained glass was set out in peerless windows, each a complete bible story, in glorious colour, which could be understood by illiterate peasants who couldn't read or write.

Some idea of the scale which generated such wealth can be gleaned from the story that contemporary monks at Gloucester had flocks of ten thousand sheep, and the monks at Tewkesbury Abbey actually had a thousand rustled. They should have acted on the text 'Watch as well as pray'!

The benefactor took good care that he should not be forgotten by posterity, because he and his wife were laid to rest, in state, beneath a magnificent carved tomb inside the church. Lesser merchants lie beneath the tombs outside, some of which are capped with huge stones, carved to resemble medieval bales of wool. No stranger can doubt what gave the surroundings such prosperity.

But I am happy to say that it is not necessary to be rich or famous to be appreciated by the good folk of Fairford today.

By coincidence, the ancient breeds of sheep which brought such prosperity to the wool merchants of the Cotswolds are still to be found in the Cotswold Farm Park, near Guiting Power.

Modern intensive husbandry and scientific genetic engineering has produced farm stock which grows faster, produces more milk per animal, and meat which has little fat to put unwanted curves on trendy housewives. The quality and flavour of the product is, alas, far down the geneticists' list of priorities, for food can now taste like cotton wool so long as it isn't sweet or fat.

Joe Henson, who keeps the Cotswold Farm Park, was in the vanguard of traditionalists who mourned the passing of ancient breeds which had been evolved by skilled craftsmen to suit the district where they farmed and the tastes of local customers.

Despite the fact that agro-tycoons rated them as sentimentalists, they formed the Rare Breeds Survival Trust, to save what was left from extinction, so we went to see it for the programme.

Until the last century, farmers took such pride in the quality of their

144

*The ancient watermill at Fairford used in the wool trade.*

stockmanship, that they vied with each other to produce individual strains of cattle and other stock which were in some way superior.

It is obvious that widely differing soils and countryside could not be ideal for every breed. The lush pastures around Uttoxeter, in the Midlands, near to where I live, are the perfect dairyland for high yield milking cows. Water meadows and the undulating, fertile slopes of Herefordshire both produce superb beef cattle. The wild hills, where we hold our trials, grow small active sheep of high quality, while the more fertile land in the lowlands will support far bigger animals such as Oxford Down, Suffolk and Border Leicester.

145

There are highly specialised breeds, such as Dorset Horn, which will breed all through the year and can produce two crops of lambs, and some of the hill breeds, such as Herdwick, whose lambs are almost black but turn grey with maturity, and produce grey, springy wool which is hard enough wearing to be ideal for carpets.

A jokester from the Wool Marketing Board once persuaded me to have a Herdwick suit, which was a lovely mixture of various shades of grey, from light to black, produced by selecting from different age groups instead of dyeing. My tailor, who is rightly proud of his quality, charged me far more to make it up than he would have done with more conventional cloth, because the wool was springy to the point of wiriness and difficult to discipline.

I discovered, when it was too late, that it is also abrasive. Where the cloth touched the tender skin of neck or upper arm, it produced sores as severe as if I had worn coarse sandpaper. John the Baptist's hair shirt would have seemed the height of luxury by comparison. I can recommend ladies troubled by hairy legs to wear a pair of Herdwick slacks. They would be more effective and cheaper than electrolysis.

In these boring days of standardisation, it is astonishing to discover that about forty quite separate breeds of sheep can still be commercially viable. All have been selectively bred for soft wool or wiry wool, long wool or short. Some produce very rapidly growing early lambs, as Hampshire Downs do, some thrive in rough country, as Scottish Blackfaces. Lonks and Herdwicks naturally 'heft' or settle to their own territory without any need for fences.

Although so many breeds survive, there was real danger that more ancient breeds, from which modern sheep are descended, would be allowed to die out because of lack of market for their produce.

Joe Henson farms a large acreage near Guiting Power, in the Cotswolds. He had about thirty five acres of land which was difficult to cultivate with modern machinery because there was too much stone near the surface, which butchered ploughs and discs and mowing machines. So, long before the trendy term 'Farm Diversification' was coined, Joe decided to diversify and keep threatened stock such as Gloucester Old Spot pigs, and Gloucester cattle which excelled for making cheese.

Countrymen of a like mind jumped on the wagon and the Rare Breeds Survival Trust was formed with the object of saving poultry and pigeons and farm stock which was dying on its feet for lack of viable commercial demand.

146

The Cotswold Farm park is now the focus of such interest, and, besides exhibiting examples of rare breeds of cattle and pigs and poultry there, a fascinating collection of sheep is on display. It is not just an exhibition of ancient breeds whose original qualities have been surpassed by careful selective breeding. The rare breeds at the Cotswold Farm Park have been widely distributed among private members of the Rare Breeds Survival Trust to provide a most important 'gene bank', which can be used as outcrosses when it becomes important to fix or reintroduce characteristics which are dying out of modern breeds or are demanded by changing fashion.

It provides a fascinating thumbnail sketch of the whole evolution of domestic sheep, including the little brown Soay sheep, no more than two feet high at the shoulder, with curved horns and 'felty' wool which was not shorn but plucked, either from the fleece or from gorse and thorn bushes where the sheep had grazed. This was such menial women's work that it is thought to have originated the term spinster.

Be that as it may, the association between man (or woman!) and Soay sheep seems to hark back to neolithic times, for small bones, which could have been Soay, and felty cloth remnants which could have been produced by contemporary spinsters, have been found in New Stone Age burial mounds, or barrows.

Soay sheep have changed down the ages less than the spinsters who collect and weave their wool. They have not yet acquired the instinct for herding, and split up and scatter when alarmed, instead of bunching, as is usual with domesticated breeds.

They don't have effete matriarchal societies, gaffered by ewes (or women!), as is the modern custom. Soay sheep run with the ram all the year round, in small social groups, each jealous of its territory.

Even more remarkable is another island breed, the North Ronaldsay sheep, thought to have been brought to the Orkneys by the Vikings, who brought other horned breeds as milk and meat on the hoof. The North Ronaldsays were landed on the inhospitable island shore, where grazing must have been sparse to the point of starvation, so they may well have made a virtue of necessity and started eating seaweed to keep body and soul together. They grew so addicted to the salty plant that they now prefer it to grass, and when some were taken to Joe Henson's farm they had to be inoculated against common diseases to which they had never been exposed, and given seaweed to supplement their diet until they tumbled to the fact that more conventional pasture can be equally satisfying.

The whole collection of these little horned sheep, many of which kill out as mutton of the very highest quality, are a great contrast to the huge Cotswold and even larger Portland sheep, which looked as big as donkeys and provided immense quantity which paid for such medieval status symbols as Fairford Church, where even the cat has a tombstone. The most satisfying thing to me is that the tycoonery of modern intensive husbandry hasn't yet managed to standardise sheep, so that small hill sheep and huge lowland hunks of animated mutton still manage to survive.

The type of hill country where primitive breeds beloved by the Rare Breeds Survival Trust could survive could be very wild indeed.

Opinions on what is or is not beautiful differ, as I discovered when our trial ground happened to border a wild hill common, which was divided from privately owned farmland by a wire netting fence. On the common side of the fence, there was a thick bracken except where stony ground made even bracken unthrifty. 'Our' side of the fence, the farmer had sprayed the bracken with Asulam, which is produced specifically to kill bracken, which should be sprayed on fine days in July. There is no apparent effect the season it is treated, but bracken simply fails to appear the following year. The farmer who owned our trials ground had sprayed his bracken the previous year and sowed a mixture of grass for permanent pasture the spring before we arrived.

The contrast could not have been starker as the camera picked out the golden hues of autumnal bracken on one side of the fence and succulent, fresh green grass on the other. It filled my eyes with admiration so that I enjoyed sharing with viewers my satisfaction that all sprays are not lethal to wildlife and that, used with discretion, they could make the desert bloom.

I should have known better. Several viewers wrote to tell me what a philistine I was to gloat over the demise of 'glorious, autumn tinted fern (sic!) to be replaced by boring, money-grubbing grass'.

Beauty may be in the eye of the beholder, but my bet is that sheep forced to scratch a miserable living from the rocky, barren, overgrazed common, would have pawned their fleeces for the chance to gorge on the succulent herbage on the other side of the fence.

On another occasion, waiting in the still September air for the first trial to begin, I heard the mournful music of hounds in full cry somewhere in the hills above me and, within seconds, a pack of Fell Hounds appeared in full cry a quarter of a mile away.

They were the traditional, copybook vision of the whole pack so

148

well bunched that a double sheet would have covered them, all with heads down to catch the scent, all singing canine hymns of hate for old Charlie Fox who was not too far ahead. I was tempted to describe the scene in purple prose, but discretion is the better part of valour, so I held my peace. *One Man and His Dog* is a programme which we wish all our viewers to enjoy, in part because it is gentle and wholesome enough to give offence to no-one.

But countrymen, especially in hill country, where small sheep are left to lamb on their own, as nature intended, are only too well aware what happens to lambs if the fox happens to interrupt the moment of birth, especially if two lambs are born. If the fox comes while the ewe is prostrate, straining to give birth to her lamb, the temptation to 'help' her by gripping the lamb's head and heaving it free may well be overwhelming. If one lamb is already born and the ewe is more than fully occupied expelling the second, the fox may find kidnapping the first is irresistible.

In our lowland country, where ewes are lambed under cover, in yards, or in enclosures by the farm house, foxes are not a serious menace to domestic stock, though gamekeepers still snare and shoot them for depleting pheasants.

Even when sheep are lambed out in the fields there are usually enough protective ewes to gang up against Charlie if he has designs on a newborn lamb while its mother is fully occupied giving birth to the second twin. Foxes will scavenge the afterbirth, on such occasions, or scoff any stillborn lambs which are left about, but they do little or no serious damage, and no-one grudges carrion.

It is very different where sheep are left on their own to lamb in isolation in the hills. A lone ewe is utterly helpless to defend her firstborn against either fox or crows while totally occupied giving birth to the second. The crow will peck the eyes or tongue out of a lamb the moment its head appears, and a fox may take any lamb until it is strong on its feet. When the ewe has recovered, she will be more than a match for any vulpine plunderer, but serious damage can be caused in the early stages of lambing if foxes are not efficiently controlled.

Lamb carcases are sometimes doped with poison, on the grounds that there is no danger except to those with an illicit taste for lamb. This is totally illegal and unselective. Buzzards and kites and domestic cats and dogs all fancy mutton carrion, but may be perfectly innocent of attacks on living sheep. There is no excuse for using poison, and no reputable sheep farmer does so. Snares and shooting are more

*Thousands of acres of good hill country could not be farmed without good dogs.*

acceptable, but the traditional, and probably most effective control of foxes, in hill country, is to hunt them with fell hounds. Such hunting is not to be confused with the rich man's ritual of the fashionable shires. This is no sport for Hooray Henrys, ponced up in pink and perched on gleaming horses. Fell hounds are hunted on foot, for the simple reason that no horse could cope with the precipitous, rocky terrain which is the habitat of hill foxes. Followers are the knowledgeable, wiry shepherds and farmers whose livelihood depends on rearing sheep. Killing foxes is business as well as sport to them, and there are no shibboleths about giving the quarry a sporting chance. If

150

the hounds mark fox to ground he is dug out with terriers and killed, as we in the lowlands would deal with rats by catching them with terriers and ferrets.

The illogical thing is that ratting with dogs and ferrets is accepted almost universally as a perfectly respectable pastime. Rats are 'vermin' and even rabid activists against 'bloodsports' do not complain about ratting.

But when I heard fell hounds hunting fox in the heights above our trial, I hesitated. My instinct warned me that prejudice against hunting is so intense that many viewers would not accept that, if they earned a hard living from sheep in the hills, they too might feel strongly when newborn lambs were savaged by foxes and that foxhounds might then become pleasantly emotive as knights in shining armour rescuing the helpless.

Whatever opinions are held about the ethics of hunting, the fact remains that shepherds in the hills regard the control of foxes as much part of protection of their flock as worming or dipping or dressing hooves against foot rot.

But I do not seek to deny that, just as sheep dogs shedding sheep are motived by a deep-rooted hunting instinct, there is also a touch of the primitive man in every shepherd following Fell Hounds. My own impulse was to hang up my microphone, say goodbye to the camera-man, and set off up the hill to join the hunt. Ian might not have approved! Nor would many viewers.

At the other end of the scenic scale was the glorious man-made scenery of Chatsworth. The tree-studded park had been laid out by the legendary Capability Brown, and now that some of his trees are passing their venerable prime, the owners plant new specimen trees to replace them. It is heartening, in these shifty times of insecurity, to discover that the Duke of Devonshire and his wife have such faith in the future that they plant young oaks to grow, for generations yet to come, so that the countryside they leave will be as beautiful for their grandchildren's grandchildren as it was for centuries past.

Some idea of just how many centuries that spans is conveyed by a visit to the Old Park. It is not open to the public, so we thought that our viewers might enjoy coming with me on a very privileged visit.

The reason it cannot be thrown open to visitors, as so much of the estate is, is that it is a very special nature reserve.

Originally, the Old Park was the outlying western edge of Sherwood Forest, and the highest rock above the Old Park is still known as Robin

Hood's seat. In an uncharacteristic moment of pessimism, Robin is supposed to have shot an arrow from this rock to decide where he should be buried. The arrow landed in the Hathersage (eight and a half miles away!), and such a demonstration of virility presumably cheered up the old rogue, because it is Little John, not Robin, who lies until eternity in the churchyard there!

What excited me, and I hope our viewers, about the Old Park, was the atmosphere of antiquity. Truly gigantic ancient oaks are dotted all around, some squat and stunted by age, with boles of twenty five or thirty feet in girth. When one was blown down and sent to the sawpit, after the last war, a ball shot was found embedded in the timber. There had been four hundred annual rings growth since the shot became embedded, and since there seemed as many inside the point where it was found, a thousand years seemed a fair estimate of the tree's age.

It is silent up there, except for the cries of woodpeckers and nuthatches, and many of the gnarled old hulks seem to have no more than a few handfuls of leaves surviving to keep them alive. It is an awe-inspiring example of tenacity to life, which fills me with faith in the future.

Tidy foresters, conscious that such ancient oaks have long since passed their prime, would have sweaty palms, itching for their axes and chainsaws to chop them down and plant commercially viable crops to replace them. The Duke of Devonshire has greater respect for the arboreal elders on his estate, so that no oak tree in the Old Park is ever felled. They are left to die in dignity and to rot and return to the earth which gave hospitality to the acorns which sired them a millenium ago.

As a result, the whole park is rich in beetles and other insects which can only make their home in the specialised habitat which has never been defiled by agricultural sprays and pesticides which have been so lethal to the friends as well as the foes in the countryside.

The air up there is pure and equally undefiled by industrial haze, so that the patina of the ancient trees is enriched by lichens of every shade of green and grey, which could not survive in the lee of most industrial cities.

Partly because people are among the rarest fauna up there, both red and fallow deer love it, and half an hour's patient immobility is rewarded when shy deer appear from nowhere and graze, oblivious of rare human voyeurs, in the clearings in the wood. Butterflies and moths, specific to natural woodland, are everywhere in warm summer weather, the moths appearing when butterflies settle for the night.

Left alone, such pleasures could only be transitory, for the sad truth is that most of the venerable oaks are past their prime, so the Duke causes about thirty-five young specimens to be planted annually to replace them when they go. The originals, of course, were planted without pre-planning – by God, and red squirrels perhaps. But the young ones, though sited with care, are in no serried ranks, beloved by formal park keepers. They are quite deliberately sited to grow naturally as near as possible to where their predecessors stood, so that, in generations as yet unborn, the Old Park of the future will be indistinguishable from the Old Park of the past; a truly natural forest which owes nothing to profit but everything to the deep respect of landowners for the land they and their family love.

Not, of course, that the estate at Chatsworth is run on sentimental lines, because if it was not efficiently managed, it would have disintegrated for lack of viability. Management is strictly commercial, producing profitable farm crops and stock and timber. While the oaks in Old Park were dozing away the centuries, such fine timber was growing in managed woodland that some of the oaks were chosen from here to replenish the oak in the roof of York Minster after it had been stricken by lightning – and only the finest timber in the land was used in that prestigious task.

We have used such illustrations as background to our sheep dog trials because our experience has proved that viewers who appreciate glorious scenery admire wise sheep dogs and enjoy the company of our delightful shepherds, are equally interested in the background of their lives.

We have lots of quiet fun ourselves, which it would be inappropriate to include in our programme, though the very fact that we enjoy our work, instead of regarding it as a chore, seems to spill over into the living rooms of our viewers.

Chatsworth was an offbeat course because conventional sheep dog trials usually entail sending the dog to a high point of the course to collect the sheep and bring them down to a pen near the spectators, as he would bring sheep down from the hills to the farmstead when shepherding the flock at home.

It made a delightful change to watch sheep being worked in such glorious man-made parkland, so we went the whole hog, built the release pen down by the river and 'fetched' the sheep up quite a steep slope to spectators standing high enough to get superb panoramic views across to another picturesque estate owned by the Devonshire's neighbour, the Duke of Rutland.

Eric and I have to do interviews and pieces to camera at widely different parts of the course, and the whole terrain was so steep and 'banky' that there was real risk that we would be out of breath when we arrived at the next location, and waste valuable camera time while we were recovering enough to be comprehensible. Always a stickler for pre-empting such avoidable porridge, Ian hired a small, amphibious multi-wheeled vehicle such as deerstalkers use to bring venison down from the hill. It will literally go anywhere, including water, leaving conventional vehicles at the starting post.

One of the stage managers that year had an irrepressible and infectious sense of humour. She was universally and affectionately known as Big Sal and, being the sort who will take on any job too arduous for lesser fry, Big Sal got lumbered with being pilot of the Argocat, which was the trade name of our go-anywhere conveyance.

*Big Sal and her 'Agrocrap' at Chatsworth.* Left to right *on offside Eric, me, Tot Longton and Big Sal. Keith and Caroline Hatton at back.*

Rides with Big Sal in her Argocat were a coveted but daunting experience. There seemed nowhere it wouldn't go – without the slightest reduction in speed, which was never less than flat out. Its eight wheels were so close together that they seemed as flexible as tank tracks, which treated ditches and hummocks, boulders and impenetrable bracken, with utter contempt. No multi-million pound ride at Disneyland could compete for sheer belly-griping thrill, so that the vehicle went down to posterity as Big Sal's Agro-crap, for it turned strong men's bowels to water. She was indeed a masterful driver.

Its claim to being amphibious was never put to the test, so Big Sal and I plotted to drive it over the river bank to land in mid-stream with the sort of splash that must have spouted heavenwards when the man went over Niagara in a barrel.

My one regret about that lovely sojourn at Chatsworth was that news leaked out about our intentions and, since Ian Smith was ultimately responsible for the safe return of all equipment he had hired, he jumped on the idea from a great height and squashed it. Big Sal and I might have been regarded as expendable, but her Agro-crap was too expensive for his budget to replace.

Some competitors are just as irrepressible and just as much fun. Charlie Relf, a tough farmer with strong views about having the National Trust as landlord, is the last chap on earth one would suspect as being into pop music. Yet he and his son Harry run a dance band which is top of the charts at all the local hops in the hill country where they farm, near Borrowdale.

Harry, his son, despite such rumbustious tastes, is a mine of information about local sheep farming traditions and customs. He produced an old pair of hand shears (or clippers) and demonstrated, with unself-conscious vigour, precisely how sheep were – and sometimes still are! – held while they are clipped with such fearsomely lethal hand shears. The great advantage over modern, mechanised machine clipping, is that a short stubble of fleece is left, standing proud of the skin, which is just enough to give reasonable weather protection until the new fleece starts to grow. With hyper-efficient machine clipping, which is not as much quicker as you might imagine, the skin is left bare enough to leave the animal tender to sun and wind and rain.

When sheep were clipped by hand it was a great social occasion at which everyone gathered. Community spirit at its best, with no political overtones. Each farm had a day for clipping and all the neighbours gathered with their dogs and implements.

155

*Charlie Relf and me. He is a distinguished triallist and judge at trials. He was our host farmer at Ullswater. He and his son run a local dance band, which is in great demand at local Lakeland functions and there is never a dull moment in company with either of them!*

The first job was to round up the sheep and bring them down to the farmstead from the hill. Then a whole row of shearers sat, each on his own clipping stool, while the younger members of the party caught the sheep and supplied each craftsman with a victim as soon as he finished the last.

Harry Relf painted the scene brilliantly in mime, settling an imaginary sheep on its back between his legs, holding it with one hand and clipping with the other, and providing vivid running commentary.

The women made clipping cake, and the sort of rural goodies which are supplied to guests by the Women's Institute, which still values quality in cooking so much more highly than purveyors of the 'convenience' junk food foisted on the unsuspecting customers of modern supermarkets.

Such hard work became an excuse for a wonderful party, the social highlight of the year, and when all the sheep were sheared at one farm, the whole concourse migrated to the next for a repeat performance.

*Harry Relf and me on a sheep clipping stool. He is a marvellous raconteur and is about to spiel off his ritual way of counting sheep. I look as if counting sheep might keep me awake instead of sending me to sleep.*

Harry Relf's enthusiasm was legendary, and he was totally unconscious of the camera, a short five feet away. He needed no prompting to demonstrate the traditional method of counting sheep, which owed nothing to computer science – 'and all that jazz' – and very little to any language known to me.

He explained that sheep were traditionally counted by the score in a lingo which began 'Yan, Tan, Tethera, Nethera, Skint,' and phrases as quick fire as an auctioneer's phoney bids up to twenty, when a notch was scored on a stick by a penknife. This was a score. A stick with five notches signified a hundred sheep.

Such arithmetical gymnastics filled Harry with more and more enthusiasm, the faster his tongue-twisting stocktaking monopolised the microphone and the camera lens. I felt I should never endure another sleepless night if I learned to recite Harry's 'Yan, Tan, Tethera, Nethera, Skint,' for my eyes would be glued in slumber long before enough sheep filed past to be recorded by the first notch to clock up a score!

# 6
# Murphy's Law
# Confounded

Murphy WAS A MYTHICAL Irishman, who had less attractive names because he expounded an immutable law which states 'what can go wrong will go wrong'.

It is a daunting prospect for anyone involved in working either with animals or television because animals are notoriously unpredictable and the more sophisticated technical equipment becomes, the greater the potential for breakdown.

My introduction and wind-up to each programme, irreverently known by my producer as 'topping and tailing', are terrifying highlights to me. If they come off, viewers are deluded into thinking that I am totally relaxed and spontaneously at home in front of cameras. They tell me that I am obviously enjoying myself, some believing that there is nothing more to it than wandering round where they would like to be on holiday, chatting to competitors about whatever crosses my mind.

They have no idea how perilously easy it would be for my mind to be a blank!

We decide at our meeting the previous evening upon the facts viewers may wish to know before we begin next day. Where the trials are being held, for viewers who have not seen previous programmes – or didn't notice what I said last time; which competitions and dogs will be competing and what the weatherman on the wireless predicted (not that what he predicts often bears much relationship to reality in hill country).

Viewers also like some hint about the magazine items which will be included, such as demonstrations of crookmaking or interesting

*Boards with complicated patterns appear in odd places. They are sited so that a nearby camera can pan round onto them to check that focus is precise.*

bygones or shepherds lambing ewes or shearing sheep. The list of permutations to go into introductions is endless.

All this would be fine if I was a professional actor and was capable of learning my lines but that is not among my accomplishments. The best I can do is to set out a list of topics in fairly logical sequence so that, if I can remember the first, the subsequent ones will prompt themselves. The result is that, if I am required to do my speel more than once, no two efforts are precisely the same, but luckily, the whole crew understand that I am just an old countryman and make allowances they would deny to professional actors.

To give Murphy every possible chance to prove his law is accurate, I am often placed in unlikely or impossible situations. I am not in the habit of standing up alone in remote countryside to harangue a non-existent audience, but Keith Hatton takes delight in causing me to pose with stunning scenery behind me and dramatic hills on one or both flanks without another soul in sight.

Three yards in front of me, eyeball to eyeball, as it were, the glassy unwinking lens of a television camera gazes contemptuously into my eyes. Behind the cameraman is an assistant cameraman. It is possible to follow the director's wishes to alter focus from a full length, distant portrait of me to a close-up of my phizog which obliterates the whole attractive landscape.

There is also a sound engineer on tap, in case my microphone packs up in mid-speech or rustles against my harsh tweed jacket – or doesn't work at all. There will be a couple of riggers to move the camera, in case the director decides on some quite different shot; an electrician to provide subsidiary lighting if clouds obscure the sun, and a man with a reflector board, which he uses like a boy-scout's heliograph, if the sun is shining – but in the wrong direction. Quite a gallery, in total, which innocent victims might assume to be a real 'live' audience, agog to catch every word the presenter had tried to memorise as he dropped

*Andrew Preston* (left) *and Christie Swan* (right) *the two judges in Ian's high observation tower from where they can watch the whole trial visually and on screen.*

off to sleep and sweated over from dawn to breakfast time.

I have been around too long to fall for that. I know that, however tolerant and charming a crew may be, they have heard it all before and are not really interested in what presenters say but only how long they will keep everyone around while they are saying it. I once let my eye stray from the camera lens and discovered that, although quite a few folk were hanging around, *nobody* was listening to what I said. The director, in his scanner hundreds of yards away may have been, but I couldn't see him. It was exactly like giving a lecture to a large audience and suddenly discovering that you'd 'lost' them; that honeyed words were falling on deaf ears because everyone had switched off. The inevitable result was that I dried up as completely as if a hostile crowd had given me the bird.

But Murphy does not rely only on chaps in camera shot to push sanity over a cliff. The weather can also be an invaluable ally, especially in the wild hill country where we work because the rainfall there is often double the amount in flatter, less dramatic scenery.

The first opening to the first programme in a new series is obviously important. If it comes off, old viewers may look forward to eight weeks with delightful men and dogs which left nostalgic memories from the last series. If the opening lacks appeal, old viewers may try something else while newcomers write it off unseen.

The beginning of the thirteenth series was especially exciting to me because I knew that the final, in eight weeks time, would be our hundredth programme, stretching back to 1975, so I did not dot all my 'i's and cross my 't's, in the hope that a truly spontaneous welcome would fit the bill.

Keith Hatton set me up, with my back to Esthwaite Water, a little jewel of a lake between Windermere and Coniston Water. Langdale Pikes towered over the far horizon. Nobody could fault the background scenery. It took quite a while to shuffle the camera into the precise spot to give the shot the director wanted but at last Keith muttered that the tape was up to speed and so he gave me the signal to do my stuff. It came off without a hitch.

Unfortunately Murphy had been eavesdropping so, within a few seconds Keith said 'Sorry, you'll have to do that again. There was a fault on sound,' and in due course he gave the cue to do it again.

There was another fault somewhere in the system. And another and another. Rain the previous night had seeped into a cable junction, screwing the picture on the camera, to add to the troubles on sound.

When the camera fault was eventually traced and cured, there was another technical hitch on sound so that I was required to do the opening five times before the director 'bought' it.

Standing alone on the shore of a lake, spouting to an impassive camera lens is not easy the first time. The fifth time round it is quite enough to sap the confidence of better men than me, though it is an integral part of television. The best that could be said for it was that I started the series five-love and Keith assured me that I could make a fluff five times before honours – or dishonours – would be even.

Old Murphy soon saw to that. I stopped counting after I was seven-five down, but I never cease to thank my stars for giving me Keith as a stage-manager. He is the kindest chap and, when I know that I have cocked it up, he always says 'Not your fault, old chap. Something wrong with sound, so they want you to do that again!'

He needn't have worried because I am fairly tough so I get stuck-in and have another go which is usually all right since I work best under pressure.

Although he is so kind and helpful, there is an iron fist beneath his velvet glove. It is obviously too time-consuming to move a camera physically every time I am required to do a link so they try to pick a neutral background where I can work simply by pivotting a camera round away from the trials course.

In one series there was a convenient spinney between the camera and a lake and Keith ushered me onto a prearranged spot to do a quick connecting link between two sequences when we were particularly hard pressed for time.

When the cameraman lined up his shot it was noticed that two strangers were standing directly in view, shattering the atmosphere of rural solitude.

Keith waved his arm, in a courteous signal to request them to move over a few yards to leave the field of vision clear. They stayed rooted to the spot, so he asked, politely, if they would move over a little as we were making a television programme and they were 'in shot'.

Normal people would have been only too happy to oblige but the male woolly hatted wanderer shouted back that they had come to watch what happened.

*Keith keeps me informed as camera lines-up for initial introduction to series.*

(Top) *Keith Hatton waves the white flag as a signal to field staff to bring the next batch of sheep from release pen to post to start next trial.*

(Right) *Keith waves red flag. Very rare, but used when a run is to be aborted for something beyond control of competitor. In this case sheep bolted from post before the signal was given to the shepherd to start the trial. It would have been unfair to judge the dog's performance against dogs which had the benefit of an unruffled bunch at the start of the trial.*

We really were pressed for time and the invective from the scanner was buckling the cable to Keith's ears, but he showed no reaction whatever. He simply walked quietly over to our uninvited guests, bade them 'Good morning', explained that we were televising a sheepdog trial and suggested that they would be welcome to join our spectators behind the rope but that they were spoiling the shot where they were.

The man said that they had come to watch what was happening and that they were staying put. He was obviously the type of bloody minded hiker who would insist on his right to follow a path through a private garden in the middle of a wedding reception on the lawn.

Still totally unruffled, Keith explained that the public footpath was on the far side of the spinney, along the side of the lake, so that if they didn't wish to join our invited guests, he would be obliged if they would follow the path because, at present, they were trespassing on private farmland.

'It isn't your farm, is it?' demanded our gawper, obviously prompted by Murphy. 'No,' Keith cooed. 'But the farmer is just over there. I'll fetch him. He's a bloody big farmer too.' It was an exception to Murphy's Law for the blots on our landscape slunk off without putting the matter to the test.

Such arrogant intruders are fortunately rare and that couple were the only example of deliberate obstruction we have encountered in our hundred programmes, but Murphy is generous with other forms of unsolicited participation in our trials.

A loose dog joining in to 'help' the competitor's dog is the nightmare we fear most but, so far, it has never happened. A hazard, perhaps, for somewhere in our next century?

Low flying aircraft can be a nuisance because they are so totally unexpected, so one of the criteria for choosing a site, is to try to avoid their regular, predictable routes. And the RAF is more cooperative than intruding hikers in making temporary diversions when necessary. Ordinary commercial traffic by aircraft can be very difficult because they are within earshot so long, starting with a low hum, no louder than a bumble bee, rising to a crescendo and gradually subsiding till the sound fades away.

This is now such a common sound, even in the most peaceful countryside that it passes almost unnoticed. The snag is that when it is necessary to edit a whole chunk out of a sequence, the background hum does not rise and fall gradually and progressively. Where the edit is made there is a *sudden* rumble or a *sudden* silence where the tape is

*Eric does his titles shot, which is mute but goes at front of each programme with titles.*

joined, which is very difficult to camouflage and which draws attention to an edit which would otherwise have passed unnoticed.

Ian Smith is such a perfectionist that the smallest of such blemishes grate on him intolerably. There are often close-up shots of the sheep going round the course, sometimes over loose stony scree, which would rattle, or through a stream, which is churned-up by their hooves or in undergrowth, which quite obviously rustles against their fleeces.

The camouflaged cameras which take the shots are usually too far away for a microphone to pick-up the sound of the sheeps' movement so that although they are seen in situations where they obviously make some noise, no sound accompanies their passage which can only be covered by general background 'atmosphere'.

This rankled with Ian who dreamed up the idea of fitting a microphone to the red collar of the sheep destined to be separated in the shedding ring.

The ruse worked fine. When sheep go through a stream, in close-up shot, the synchronised sound of splashing feet gives the illusion of being with them on their trials circuit. Loose pebbles scattered when

166

they go across the bare scree of remote hillsides prompts thoughts about just how tough their horny feet must be to withstand such treatment as they crop their daily living. But Murphy had his joke as well!

Sheep are ruminants, and they do not simply pluck grass, swallow and digest it. They have an extra stomach so that they can ingest large quantities of food and then retire to 'chew their cud'. The food they have stored is simply belched back in small wadges, or 'cuds' and chewed thoroughly, at leisure, before being reswallowed for final digestion.

The red collar microphones are as sensitive to cudding belches as they are to the patter of horny hooves. At intervals in the programme, unscheduled and unexplained rude noises can be heard. They do not emanate from me, however much Murphy would like you to think so! It is simply the process of ovine digestion.

(Left) *A sound engineer fixes a microphone to one of two red collars to be fitted on sheep used in next round of trial. This microphone will pick up sounds of sheep as they are driven round the course, giving clattering hooves, over rough scree, rustle of vegetation in cover or splashing as they cross a stream. It will also give an unsolicited jumble of burps and belches as the sheep regurgitates food in order to chew the cud!!*

(Right) *The shepherd holds a sheep, chosen at random for the collar to be fitted.*

*The shepherd bringing his sheep to the release pen in the morning. Some of them will be selected at random to be released in batches of seven for separate trials later on. Two red collars, one with microphone attached, will be fitted before sending to lift post and retrieved before being turned into the exhaust pen at the end of the trial.*

We were once in trouble when Ian hired a bunch of sheep for the trials which were exceptionally wild and unmanageable because they had been bred and reared in the hills where they had been subject to minimum management.

Their owner was perfectly open about it, saying that they had no experience with dogs and, when a dog attempted to drive them, they would probably bolt like hares. But he promised that 'they would be all right on the night!'

So, a fortnight before our trials he brought down a large enough flock for us to do a whole day's work using a fresh bunch for each trial but leaving a few still in the release pen. He paddocked them in fenced enclosures, which included our trials course, and moved them round every day so that they gradually became accustomed to accepting the dog as their guardian and guide, well managed, but still skittish enough to test the authority of competitors' dogs.

Murphy must have laughed his eye up! What everyone had overlooked was that, in previous series, the sheep had always been brought from neighbouring but not adjacent pastures. They had usually arrived in the morning in a cattle truck and been shut in the release pen.

When each bunch was released for a trial, they were on strange ground, not knowing where they might be driven or where their sanctuary, the exhaust pen lay. They had no incentive to run in any direction more than any other.

The sheep we blundered over had been enclosed on a few fields, including the trials ground, for two weeks and driven backwards and forwards through every gateway in exercises designed to accustom them to obeying but not fearing the dog. We only discovered the potential for disaster when we had the first trial runs, to line-up cameras, the day before the trial started.

Seven sheep were ushered out of the release pen and driven, by the field staff, gently towards the lift post. They were pretty spooky and would obviously be a tricky handful for the most experienced dog. Softly-softly-catchee-monkey tactics might work but over enthusiasm would certainly galvanise them into an uncontrollable stampede.

The non-competing shepherd who had agreed to give the demonstration runs was a master of his craft and all went well the first run. The second batch made a bolt for a gate into the next field the

*'After the trial.' Sheep turned out in next field to graze where the exhaust pen was.*

moment they had been released. So did several more, gaining sanctuary before the dog had even been dispatched on his outrun. I scented a catastrophe, for Murphy had apparently dealt his joker before a hand was played.

It took some time for the explanation to emerge. Despite being apparently tractable, when confronted by a good dog, their instinct for self preservation is still not far below the surface and their cunning is not to be underrated. When dumped in totally strange territory, even flighty sheep are fairly manageable by a good dog for the simple reason that they have no idea in which direction safe sanctuary lies.

These sheep, having been confronted by a good working dog every day in the last couple of weeks, had learned that dogs were not hungry predators, so that flight in blind panic was not the essential for survival. But they had had the time and opportunity, while the dog had been 'working' them, to learn every stick and stone, gateway and impassable wall, in the area to which they were confined, as intimately as the horn on their hooves. They retained enough of the instincts for survival of truly wild animals to make them dive for safety with the reflex of frightened rabbits and familiarity with the area had taught them where to dive.

The second batch, which bolted for the gate, knew from experience that safety from pursuit lay in the field over the fence as surely as a rabbit knows that his salvation from gnashing teeth lies just inside his warren and on familiar ground they know precisely where every warren is.

Ian made our fears crystal clear to the flockmaster but my confidence in any improvement next day was sadly shaken. I would have laid five to one on Murphy – but I am happy to confess that I would have lost my money.

The following morning sheep were trickled out of the release pen to the lift post and the demonstration run was immaculate! I couldn't make up my mind whether a completely fresh bunch of sheep had been substituted, which had not the advantage of knowing the terrain, or if someone had waved a magic wand over yesterday's rebellious rogues.

The (quite different!) truth only seeped out in driblets because real countrymen are shy about making strangers privy to the tricks of their trade.

The fact that they knew that I am a genuine 'dog-man' myself, involved with *working* dogs for more than half a century, obviously helped. And many of them have developed a mutual respect through sharing with me so many television sheepdog programmes. So they paid me the compliment of taking me into their confidence and describing the steps they took to persuade our flighty sheep to behave.

They did so only because they regard me as 'one of them' so nothing would persuade me to betray their secret to unknown readers who they might regard as impersonal outsiders!

Simple physical disability was the other battle we have had to wage with Murphy.

The first programme back in 1975 was a short film shot on the farm of Tim Longton who farms in the hills near Lancaster. Philip Gilbert, who produced the first few programmes wanted to give the flavour of things to come by introducing viewers to a competitor and his family and show what life on wild hill farms is really like.

Tim was a fine example, because he and his brothers and sons are famous for their skills at shepherding sheep. The farm is high and bleak so that, even in hot summers, it requires no flights of fancy to imagine how tough conditions can be when winter grips.

*Ian in his observation hut overlooking the course. He can see the whole course and has monitors, on which he can see what every camera has in focus and ask for changes by the director. Sharing his hut are one sound engineer, two judges, Eric and me.*

Showing it at its best, we were able to kindle nostalgic fancies of the deep satisfaction of limitless horizons, brought down to earth by close-ups of hoof-shattering scree and back cracking scrambles to get from one steep valley to the next. The film portrayed wild countryside to which those caught in the urban rat race would love to escape – in theory – however shattered by privation they would be if ever their bluff was called and they had to transform sweet dreams to harsh reality.

We showed Tim's dogs gathering sheep from precipitous fells, unclimbable by clumsy human feet and, in contrast, we were entertained in the snug comfort of the Longtons' hospitable house, with a kettle ever on the hob and home cooked food to fill voids created by unaccustomed exertions on the storm wracked hills outside. As with other top competitors we have met since then, there were rows of shining silver cups and red rosettes, tangible evidence of past successes, orphan cade lambs to be bottle reared, puppies to be fed and all the basic attractions which are fuelling the return of pressured city-slickers to the simpler ways of life of rural ancestors from the bygone past.

When we had made the film, I was requested to go to Television Centre to dub on commentary to the shortened edited sequences of silent film. The producer had a personal assistant who allowed no grass to grow under her feet because she never put both on the ground at the same time. She personified perpetual motion with a synchronised soundtrack.

I arrived five minutes before my appointment but found her waiting in reception, accusing watch in hand, as if I had committed the cardinal professional sin of being late.

Brushing aside my expostulation that I had plenty of time to spare, she informed me coldly that 'they' were waiting, so 'hurry up' with which she tripped off down endless smooth and polished corridors without waiting to see if her senior by nearly half a century was keeping up.

Trip, trip, trip down the corridors she went and trip, trip, trip down the stairs, with me trip, trip, tripping a pace or so behind her. Unfortunately the stairs were even more lethal than the passages, my feet went from under me, I passed her in full flight and landed in a huddle at the bottom.

'It hasn't hurt you,' she spat menacingly. 'Pick yourself up. They're waiting.' I picked myself up obediently and spent a miserable and painful day in the studio, dubbing sound onto silent film, and went to see a specialist at home next day. He said I had broken my arm, which didn't surprise me because I had heard it crack. He put it in a cunning splint, which was slim enough to get through the armhole of my jacket, so that the personal assistant could assist by stitching a split sleeve round it each morning the following week, when we were filming on location. By painful contortion, I could just conceal the injury by forcing my hand into my jacket pocket while I was on camera, so that I got through the first series with a newly broken but cunningly camouflaged right arm.

Having survived – and defeated – Murphy's physical assault before the first programme of the first series, back in 1975, I remained unscathed on annual expeditions till the twelfth series which we recorded in 1987. Then, a fortnight before D-day, I caught my foot in a half buried strand of wire and took a terrific purler onto a newly stoned forest ride. The jagged rocks pulverised my lower leg, blocking the blood vessels which, till then, had coped with return circulation from my foot. The result was that my foot swelled uncontrollably so that it was six months before I could get into a shoe or welly boot – but two weeks before I was due on location at Ullswater for our twelfth series. Murphy had bided his time but had pulled another fast one.

A stout thumb stick and oversize galosh gave limited, if painful mobility. Ian provided a Land Rover to convey me to the part of the course where I was next required and, when it decanted me near camera, Keith was as solicitous as a sympathetic nurse. The director took shots that never showed my unconventional footwear and viewers never rumbled my lack of mobility.

The thirteenth series was due to end with a final which fell on our hundredth programme. It may have meant nothing to outsiders, but it would be a momentous day for us – if it ever dawned! Having a some-what superstitious streak, I was none too happy about it being the *thir-teenth* programme. Determined not to tempt fate by letting the unlucky number pass my lips until it was too late, I concentrated on the prospect of five score programmes instead. You can't fool Murphy like that.

Ian had occupied much of the summer making sequences at com-petitors' homes to be inserted as 'magazine' items in due course. His quiver of varied items was almost full and he wanted a particularly dramatic scene of sheep being shepherded in their natural environment among the Black Mountains in Wales. His host, David Daniel had well managed sheep and an impeccably mannered dog. The day was perfect, the scenery magnificent. It was an aesthetic producer's dream.

173

*The awards. A salver for the runner-up and a television camera for the winner, of both singles and brace with a sash of honour presented by the International Sheep Dog Society. The plinths hold a new collar for each of the canine winners.*

The camera crew were in a rocky gully, filming dog and sheep against an almost perfect background. Ian would not be satisfied until he had made near-perfection perfect.

He edged cautiously towards the brink of the cliff above the camera crew but was still unable to visualise the shot they'd got. He inched nearer and nearer the edge, giving suggestions as each new angle hove in view. Totally absorbed, he failed to notice how little grip was provided by the wiry mountain grass. He will never know whether it was just bad luck or careless judgement or if mythical Murphy materialised to give him a sly nudge. Whatever the motivation, his feet slipped from under him and he slithered remorselessly over the brink, fetching up in a heap on a pile of boulders twelve feet below.

Now Ian is no lightweight. God built him more for comfort than for speed and even bouncy, athletic types don't tumble twelve feet onto a

174

pile of rocks with impunity. The fall shook him from stem to stern but his full weight landed at an awkward angle on his ankle, twisting and wracking the whole of his leg. Most people would have taken to their beds but his enthusiasm and dedication are such that he turned up on location as if nothing had happened.

When his patience is approaching breaking point, he grows quieter and quieter and, though normally a courteous man, he becomes even more polite. It is a symptom we have learned is ignored at our peril. The final warning, before eruption is put on the hair trigger, is when he says quietly, 'Now *Gentlemen* ...' I kick Eric's ankles and shrink into my shell, maintaining a low profile until storm signals are lowered and everything is on course again.

We noticed, while recording the thirteenth series, that there were rather more 'gentlemen' about. It was some measure of the pain and discomfort he was suffering from his toss into the gully, but I never heard him grumble once. He used a Land Rover to carry him from morning briefing to his observation hut and it decanted him at the mess tent entrance at midday. A slight superfluity of gentry foregathered at our evening conference so that light hearted, hollow jocularity fell flat. Otherwise we would never have guessed what guts it must have taken to carry on. The fact that six months later, as I write this, he is still having treatment for his damaged leg hammers home the fact that, in Ian's book, 'the show must go on – whatever the cost'. The shining example has not been lost on Eric and me. We are determined to follow suit in the next century (of programmes not years!) refusing to pack up till we have tumbled off our perches and *rigor mortis* has set in!

Such programmes inevitably balance on a perilous knife edge, threatened with dislodgement from one side by outside forces such as unmanageable sheep or peasouper fogs, physical accidents and innumerable hazards, falling within the Law of Murphy, But, like the Trojan horse, some of the perils emanate from internal ailments which in theory should be above suspicion.

*One Man And His Dog* has wide appeal to both urban and rural viewers. The pure sport of sheepdog trialling has a dedicated but tiny following of practical enthusiasts who will go through hell and high water not to miss watching themselves or their close shepherding friends competing for supremacy on the little box. As pure statistics, they are insignificant, though they are likely to derive deep and lasting satisfaction from such programmes.

A wider spectrum of country folk in general like it because, whether

*Making notes in the observation hut for interview with competitors after trial.*

they have ever owned and worked a collie or not, it is 'their' type of programme which genuinely tries to give a true and vivid picture of a way of life they live and love and understand.

They welcome programmes which have no violence or sex or smart alec thuggery. They do not rate it old hat to love England – or Scotland or Wales or Ireland! – better than gaudy foreign lands, without diet or culture in common. They are not ashamed to admit pride in being British. Knocking an 'establishment' which defends old fashioned values does not turn them on and hard-faced interviewers making 'ordinary' folk look silly fill them with embarrassment.

I have everything in common with them. My father was a family doctor with a mining practice and his patients ranged from small farmers to one large landowner, with a large number of pigeon-flying, whippet racing, miners in between. When I was young, colliers loved poaching more than picketing, and doctors knew their patients personally, in those days. They were not simple entries in a receptionist's

176

card index. When any of them were ill, from the local poacher to the squire, my father visited them himself, even if they chose Saturday night or Sunday to call him out. He did not send a strange young man who was hired as a stand-in, to cover inconvenient times.

As a result, my father's patients were my friends and I have a powerful common bond with similar countrymen at all levels of society. Most of the characters who appear in *One Man And His Dog* could so easily have been friends of my own childhood, and it is not unreasonable to suppose that what appeals to me is likely to meet their approval too.

I was broadcasting in the 1940s and '50s and worked in Lord Reith's day. He believed that the wireless would be a powerful medium which would have a powerful influence on society, and he believed that it was a tool which should be used to educate and inform and improve – as well as to amuse, but never to subvert. If he was going strong today, I believe there would be less violence and thuggery on the immoral little boxes in the corners of our sitting rooms – and

*The plan of the course made by Andy Bloomfield to show competitors, at briefing, and for use on screen to help viewers. Eric and Ian discuss.*

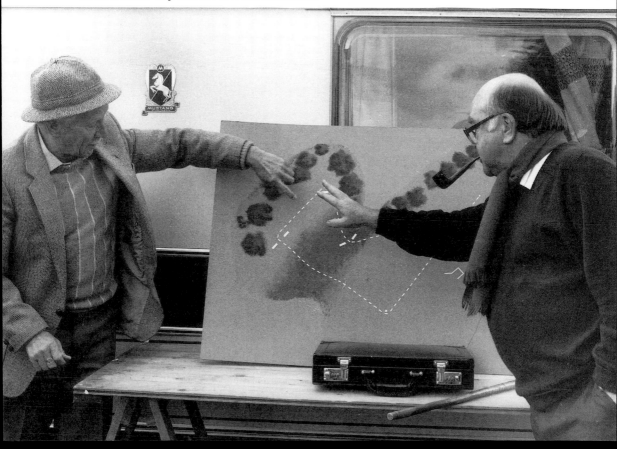

probably in the streets as well. I am not ashamed to nail my colours to his mast.

Such high falutin' notions are scoffed at by the 'intellectual' theorists who now dictate what we do or do not see, but the fact that simple, wholesome country programmes are capable of attracting a high number of viewers lends weight to my theory.

Perhaps it may be argued that the reason country folk enjoy the programme is that it is about them and their friends and we all like seeing people we know on the screen.

But townsfolk love it too and the sheer *number* of regular viewers, who switch on casually and then get hooked, come predominantly from towns.

The pace and brittleness of our competitive urban rat race is producing a torrential backwash which suggests that the answer is to 'get away from it all'.

The reason for this unstoppable surge from town to country is that the machines and modern technical 'miracles' of our computerised age threaten to become our masters instead of our slaves.

There is a widespread, overpowering nostalgia for a simpler, saner way of life. Whether or not it is an illusion, the impression is growing that our ancestors lived more naturally so that there is growing interest in traditional crafts and ancient customs. Bygone rural tools and implements which, a generation ago gathered dust in junk shops or rusted away on rubbish dumps, are now expensive, highly desirable prizes offered by fashionable dealers in antiques.

Craftsmen, building dry stone walls or shepherds, shearing sheep are no longer jokey curiosities. They perpetuate the skills of our forefathers, and are respected by our generation which is capable of little better than pressing keys on a computer. The junk 'convenience' foods, purveyed by supermarkets are now recognised as a poor substitute for the 'natural' foods of our forefathers, which were untainted by chemical pesticides or growth-promoting hormones.

Politicians, of all shades, have suddenly tumbled to the fact that there are votes waiting for the prophets in 'green' parties and the signs are that we are on the threshold of an era when governments will owe allegiance to those who put them in power from the countryside so that urban matters will have to fit in with rural wishes instead of the reverse.

This drift from town to countryside has accelerated gently for the last decade or so, coinciding with a dozen series of our television

178

sheepdog trials, which have happened to be in tune with the changing wishes of an entirely new spectrum of country dwellers, most of whom still earn their living by commuting into towns.

It was a windfall we neither foresaw, nor created so that any success which fell into the programme's lap was, as so often happens, more due to luck than judgement.

But it also happens that good luck is often engineered as well as being only due to chance. Ian Smith has deliberately set out to satisfy the sudden public thirst for a simple lifestyle, in pleasant places, by weaving into his programme a wide variety of peripheral rural topics, which have given flavour to simple sheep and sheep doggery.

Lambing and dipping in foul substances, calculated to ward off disease are by no stretch of the imagination competitive trialling but are interesting facets of a coveted way of life. Sheep bells and branding irons, shepherd's huts and horn lanterns are among the fascinating bygones collected by Gordon Beningfield, who is among the top flight of modern rural artists. What appeals to him appears in his paintings, which fetch prices which reflect just how popular such traditional customs of our ancestors have become. So Gordon is one of the most popular and regular guests on the programme because he distils, in art, what so many viewers have only been able to dream about but now see as realistic goals to include in their plans for a more civilised lifestyle.

One man and his dog, practising the skills of his ancestors, in the same wild places, with man's best friend the dog, as the only tool of the trade, appealed when we started only to the tiny band of enthusiasts who shared the same interests. Casual viewers, switching on from curiosity, enjoyed the scenery and uncanny relationship between animals and man.

The lifestyle of such a shepherd and his dog was the very antithesis of frustrating commuter jams, repetitive jobs, competitive status symbols and frightening insecurity. The vast throng which was already drifting from town to countryside instinctively latched on. By the pure luck of accidental timing, our unselfconscious shepherds have become cata-lysts to fire the imagination of hordes of townsfolk who are currently escaping urban life to flock to the countryside.

The programme is designed to be transmitted in winter evenings, when glorious autumn colours and landscape will prompt nostalgic memories. Country folk, thawing out frostbitten fingers, by cosy log fires, are just in the mood for such relaxation. Recent in-comers to the

179

countryside, the fugitives from the urban rat race, settle down, after a miserable, frustrating, foggy journey out of the big city, to the certainty that 'this' is the life they crave for; the simple, healthy lifestyle makes the hassle of coming thirty miles from work worthwhile. to meet this need, the last series was planned to begin at half past seven o'clock, starting once a week in January evenings.

This time Murphy came unstuck. He put the series off till March, each programme beginning at six pm on BBC2. His supposition was that his law, once more, would prove that things which can go wrong, will, was only too accurate. The tables turned on him! At six pm on light spring evenings, farmers are farming and commuters are commuting. It is impossible to watch TV while acting as midwife to a ewe, dairymaid to a cow or ploughing a furrow. Commuters, locked in mudguard crunching traffic jams, can concentrate only on how to survive asphyxiation by petrol and diesel fumes. Dogs shepherding their sheep in idyllic scenery are but a mirage in such stressful deserts.

The miscalculation Murphy made in changing the time and date was that countrymen, whether born-and-bred or newly arrived, do not suffer in silence. A spate of indignant letters, complaining about insensitive timing, made the matter plain.

The number of viewers slumped – for the obvious reason that their presence before their screens was physically impossible. But Murphy's suggestion that the decline was due to a shrinking audience of ageing decrepits did not hold water. He overlooked the fact that the marvels of modern science have so lengthened life expectancy that the population is not only living longer but also carrying a greater proportion of financial clout. And, since more and more people are migrating to the countryside we are rapidly becoming a rurally dominated society, no longer subject to the whims of a brittle clique of city slickers.

Conservation and 'green' issues, 'simple' lives and 'natural' foods, traditions and rituals are no longer rated old hat. They are the buzz words of the next decade and sheepdog trialling is ideally in context. The Powers-that-be in broadcasting were most kind and took the point. A better transmission time was promised for the next series.

The national press, with its sensitive finger on the public's pulse, have always been kind to the programme. Daily and national newspapers have done features about the shepherds to whom we have introduced our readers. Sunday paper magazines have splashed the sport over their whole front covers and cartoonists have had a field day.

180

We were delighted, after the series recorded at Chatsworth, to find a faithful picture of the course over the whole front and back covers of the *Giles Annual*, published by the *Daily* and *Sunday Express*.

On the front cover, Grandma glowers in glorious technicolour at three dogs, holding up a packet of sheep near a hurdle pen, while Junior, the shock headed brat, takes a close-up with his camera.

The back cover has been breathed on by Murphy because the dogs have left the sheep and 'penned' Grandma instead. She wards them off with her umbrella, while Junior records the scene for Giles-orientated posterity.

Even political and farming cartoonists take it for granted that their more general readers are well versed in the pastoral world of shepherds and their dogs.

After the Chernobyl disaster, sheep in areas where signs of radioactive fallout had been detected could not be sold for human consumption in case they had eaten contaminated pasture. Mac produced a lovely cartoon of a shepherd and his dogs, perched on the branches of a tree, with a man in a cap, who looked like me sharing their sanctuary. A bunch of aggressive looking sheep, with canine teeth, surrounded the tree, forcing the fugitives to stay aloft. The caption reads: 'I don't care what the Ministry of Agriculture says. Sheep have never been the same since Chernobyl.'

Greetings card manufacturers jumped on the wagon and even Carling Black Label produced an amusing Tele Commercial showing a shepherd and his dog with some sheep in typically wild hill country.

The shepherd commands his dog to fetch the sheep – but the dog lies down instead, though the sheep proceed through the fetch gate with nothing in sight to guide them. The next command has absolutely no effect on the dog, which simply flicks one ear without even bothering to get up, while the sheep continue on course without their canine guide.

The whole trial is completed perfectly, with the dog still at his master's feet, acknowledging commands by no more than a flick of an ear or wink of an eye – but his master wins the silver cup.

The punch line to the question 'You've got a fine dog there Jack. I bet he drinks Carling Black Label?' is 'No, Phil. Never when he's driving!' When hard headed ad-men reckon that viewers on independent channels recognise subjects transmitted only on the esoteric airwaves of BBC 2's minority channel, poor Murphy's predictions of inevitable disaster must be well off target!

For some reason – perhaps because caps are easy to caricature – many cartoonists highlight my cap, the blurb under Cole's cartoon in the *Daily Express* claiming that I had 'probably done more for the sale of cloth caps than anyone, not excluding Mark Phillips'.

Competitors always turn up respectably dressed, so Eric and I keep our end up, by wearing whatever we would wear if we went to a trial which was not being recorded on TV. I opened the first programme of the first series in a particularly favourite check tweed suit. It was not new, having been made for me in 1957, eighteen years earlier!

My view is that old suits, which were first class when they were made, in the quality of their cloth and cut and workmanship, still look better than modern mass-produced 'fashionable' trash even after they have been to the cleaners so often that they could find the way there themselves.

So the next year and the year after and the year after that, I turned up in my old check suit for the first and last programmes in each series. It became an in-joke, a sort of lucky charm which torpedoed new fangled notions that what could go wrong, would.

By the eleventh series, when my suit was just thirty years old, it began to pinch a bit so I took it to my tailor – a generation junior to the man who made it – and told him it had shrunk.

'My clients often say that,' he said, 'I'll put a gusset in it.' It fitted

*'Phil Drabble has probably done more for the sale of cloth caps than anyone, not excluding Mark Phillips.'*

perfectly that year and the next but then it began to feel a little tight again. Determined not to look as if I'd been poured into it by the hundredth programme, I took it back to my tailor and accused him of skimping his gusset because the suit was still pinching. He looked resigned and asked to see it on. 'I agree it *could* do with letting out,' he said. 'Perhaps you are still growing? Anyhow, I'll deal with it again. I've often put a gusset in for my clients – but this will be a "first" for me. I've never put a gusset in a gusset before!'

Despite the pressures involved in recording eight forty-five minute programmes in five-and-a-half days, there is nothing I would rather do, and I hope that competitors and crew feel the same. Our annual expedition to some of the wildest and most beautiful places, where we are sure to meet old friends and make new ones, with similar outlooks and tastes, is the purest form of pleasure. Working with Eric for thirteen years and Ian for ten speaks for itself. As a sop to our pride in exclusivity Ian produced an unobtrusive tie which is presented only to those who have worked directly for the programme or competed in the trial it depicts. The tie bears modest insignia which would be meaningless to the uninitiated but is greatly prized by us. A plain, small shepherd's crook has a dog's footprint one side of the shank and a sheep's cloven hoof the other. The design is completed by the letters BBCtv, small and discreet enough to be deciphered only by those already in the know. It means as much to us as a Guards' or Old Etonian tie means to those who gyrate in more exalted circles.

The pleasure of being involved in creative work with such enthusiastic professionals would be hard to beat. I have enjoyed myself so much that there has never been a period in my life which I would willingly have swapped for any period which has gone before. Each has been even better than the last. I hope my luck will hold until the day I tumble off my perch.

# Index